The Race Of A
LIFETIME

The Race Of A
LIFETIME

A True Story About Running, Abuse, Rebellion,
Forgiveness, and God's Pursuit of a Man

Michael Layne

authorHOUSE®

AuthorHouse™
1663 Liberty Drive
Bloomington, IN 47403
www.authorhouse.com
Phone: 1-800-839-8640

Published by AuthorHouse   05/23/2012

ISBN: 978-1-4772-0379-8 (sc)
ISBN: 978-1-4772-0378-1 (e)

Library of Congress Control Number: 2012908691

DEDICATION

This book is dedicated back to my Lord and Savior, Jesus Christ. Without Him this would have not been possible.

This book is also dedicated to all of my nieces and nephews.

With Love from Uncle Mike,

"I'm in constant prayer for each of you. I pray as future men and women you seek and keep Christ in the center of your lives. He's the <u>Only</u> foundation that will never break. Keep standing and relying on Him." I love you all.

Contents

Acknowledgments ix
Preface..xiii

Chapter 1 1
Chapter 2   The Blessing: An Open Door to
                 America 3
Chapter 3   Public Hiding Place 14
Chapter 4   St. Paul, Minnesota between
                 1988 to1989 23
Chapter 5   Stability 2 31
Chapter 6   The Set Up: Bailly Middle School......... 40
Chapter 7   Entering Cougar Territory 50
Chapter 8   On My Own... 58
Chapter 9   Boys Will Be Boys 68
Chapter 10   The Finish Line of Senior Year
                 1995-1996... 83
Chapter 11   Crowned King 101
Chapter 12   The First Moments at the University
                 of Iowa 115
Chapter 13   The University of Iowa's NCAA
                 Cross Country Team Appearance
                 (Fall 1998) 131
Chapter 14   Life Goes On 140
Chapter 15   Back to Minnesota.............................. 146

Chapter 16	Going to Panama June 2002	152
Chapter 17	Back Home in Minnesota	164
Chapter 18	Plan Predicted	172
Chapter 19	The Brewing of God's Plan	178

Acknowledgments

First and most of all, I give all honor and praise to my Lord and Savior Jesus Christ, who fully set me free when He died on the cross and paid the price for all of my sins. One day I will be with Him forever in heaven. My faith tells me so. I deserve nothing, but God loved me so much that He sacrificed His only Son for me. Jesus is God's gift to the entire world. I thank you Lord! This book is dedicated right back to You.

God gave me the vision to write this book for two main purposes. The first purpose is to show how He's orchestrated my life for His glory. The second purpose is to share the Gospel of Jesus Christ. This book is a door-opener for me to share my faith to many.

I want to share my prayer with you.

> Lord, I am not sure who this book is intended for, but I pray that You let it have its way because it's You who inspired me to write it. You set it up from the beginning. Lord, I battled with You. I was afraid of so many things including writing this book but You told me to keep pressing on. Satan has been at work. He's currently at work coming after me, but You keep saying, "Press on."
>
> Your word has been my comfort during this book writing process, and You're not done with shaping me. You have put too much

inside of me that has to come out. You have revealed so much to me, and I'm not a failure in Your eyes. I can't be silent about You. I can't be ashamed to tell people about You. I can't run from You anymore.

You're awesome Lord! Why do You love me (a sinner) so much, I'll never understand, but I'm thankful You do. I am grateful You didn't turn Your back on me as I did You. The same way You came to me, I pray You give others a chance, too. Show others Your glory. Thank You for using me to help reach others. I say all these things, in Jesus name. Amen!

The acknowledgement section is the part of the book where I had the most trouble. Why? There are so many people God placed in my life that I have to thank. I wanted to thank everyone individually (each one of you knows who you are). The reality is that it would take a long time, and I could possibly miss thanking someone in the process. So I chose to make my acknowledgements general but most of all, genuine. Thank you to: all of my family, friends, peers, pastors, coaches, teachers, mentors, churches, singers, schools, co-workers, Brothers, the city of Gary along with other cities etc. etc. etc. Seriously, the list goes on. Thank you to my family in Barbados and Panama.

I want to thank my Walgreens family on 43rd and Broadway Street. Also my track teammates from high school and college. Though my godfather George McBean wasn't in the book, he was a major part of my life. I just want to send a special dedication to him for being a constant provider.

I am thankful for the people God placed in my path. Some people were there for a split second, some helped shaped me, and some people are currently with me on my journey now. But through it all, everyone served and serves a purpose.

I am truly amazed at what God has done, can do, and will do in the future. No matter what is going on, my sights are set on Him even when the clouds get dark. In the Bible there are countless examples of how God shows up in the wilderness and gets His glory. I can't be afraid any longer. I know that God is with me. To the people I have let down, I ask and seek your forgiveness.

To the people who let me down, all is forgiven. I am continually seeking Christ, and He's taught me that I can give everything to Him. I have given everything to Him. He's forgiven me, and now I follow Him to help save someone else. That's my mission and I pray that as believers in Him, we all make it our mission.

Preface

> And we know that God causes all things to work together for good to those who love God, to those who are called according to His purpose. For those whom He foreknew, He also predestined to become conformed to the image of His Son, so that He would be the firstborn among many brethren; and these whom He predestined, He also called; and these whom He called, He also justified; and these whom He justified, He also glorified.
>
> Romans 8: 28-30 (NASB)

If you would have told me I would write a book about my life and the love of God just to inspire at least one person in this world, I would have wondered if something was wrong with you.

Writing has never been my strength, and at many points in my life, neither was talking about God. In fact, the minute someone would talk about God to me in depth, I would find some way to escape hearing the information. I was good at running, so I would literally run in the opposite direction when anything about God came up. I didn't want to hear it.

It's enough to make me laugh when I look at my past. I was blind to God. I had no idea seeds were being planted in me during my life, and that God would eventually grab my attention. No matter how I continued to turn my back on God, He knew when He would come to me.

There are many Christian inspirational books designed to help and inspire people to change their lives. How can telling a snippet of my life help someone else? This was the main question I repeatedly asked God when He placed it on my heart to write this book. Why use me? I'm no better than the next person. I'm a work in progress, and according to God's standards, I still fall short.

How can I tell someone about the greatness of God when I am flawed? I have made a lot of bad choices and some horrible mistakes. I've been hurt, and I hurt a lot of people. In fact, there was a point in the wilderness of my mind where I thought about throwing in the towel. So why would God want to use a sinful man like me?

Now, I can boldly answer these questions and more just by reading the word of God. Before I share my journey with you, I will say God is amazing! Many times I've said this just to go along with everyone else. I had no idea that I would experience these words and share them with others now and forever. God revealed to me that my life's story was meant to glorify Him and to help someone else get to know Him.

My life does have meaning and purpose for God. I could not be here without His favor on my life, especially with all that I have done. Someone out there needs to know that his or her life has purpose for God. He really wants to have a solid relationship with us, even with all of our flaws.

Whomever this book is intended for, God does not want you to give up. He's in control even when you don't see a way out. Of course there will be trials and tribulation in life, but God is in the midst of all that's taking place. As you'll read you will see that many times I did things my way, but God had another plan for me. He saw more than I could see. In fact, He sees more than any of us can see. After all, He is the creator of the heavens and the earth. He knows what is best for us. He gave us The Answer, and that's Jesus Christ. I am a witness that if you totally submit your life to Christ, just as you are, He will transform you. He's gradually doing it for me each day. My life is finished in Him. Here's my short journey. "On your marks. Get set. Go!"

CHAPTER 1

The ground was hard under my feet. I casually walked the marked path instead of taking off in my usual gazelle like run. One of the most important days of my life would unfold at the place I felt most familiar with. I have always been a runner. In the beginning I was only running from someone or somewhere. Eventually, I began to run for competition. On the track with me there have always been either fellow teammates spurring me to do better as they trained with me or competitors doing their job to beat me to the finish line.

Today was different. My companion on the track was not the kind of teammate that I'd spent grueling hours with training, joked with on long bus rides to far away meets, or who fought hard with me toward many finish lines of my life. Neither was this person a daunting figure from the past causing my heart to race and sweat to break out across my forehead in fear.

Even though I knew I could trust the footsteps walking in unison with mine more than I'd ever dared to trust anyone, I was terrified. All the old questions and doubts had their own race around my mind. *Would I fail? Was I good enough?* Hopes battled with insecurities.

Before we completed a lap on the track, I sensed the impatience of my companion. I knew I had to act. As usual, I could see the finish line but it was not coming fast enough. Once we reached the finish line I knew this was where God wanted me to be. I was at the right place at the divine time.

This was it! I tuned out all the fear-soaked voices in my head, attempted to calm my pounding heart, and said the one sentence I never imagined would come out of my mouth.

CHAPTER 2

THE BLESSING:
AN OPEN DOOR TO AMERICA

If I had to compare my life as a child to something, it would be like a sprint. There were numerous short races I ran in, got pulled out of then placed in another race. My life's sprint started in Panama before I was born. My mother Laura lived there until she was given the opportunity to come to the United States by her godmother, Estelle. My mother's decision to join Estelle would soon change my life.

When Estelle came to work in the United States in 1977 she took her first income tax check to sponsor my mother to join her. Laura was sixteen years old. She was also six months pregnant with me and she wanted a better life in the United States. At the time the airlines did not allow pregnant women to fly to avoid medical risks. This caused my mother to decide to wear a big sweater, which hid her pregnant condition. On September 7, 1977 at 3:45 p.m. I came into the world.

I was born at St. Francis Hospital in Evanston, Illinois, just three months shy of being born in Panama. And although, my father, Pedro Avila, would never get the chance to visit the United States or witness my birth, my mother said he was excited he was having a child.

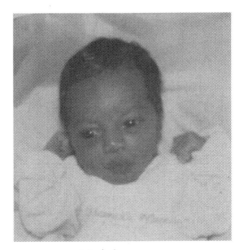

My baby picture

Me 1 year old

Growing Up Fast

My mother was a teenage parent, having me just two months shy of her seventeenth birthday. She had a lot to learn about being an American. The beauty of it all was that as she was learning and I would be learning with her.

I wish I could recall everything that took place in my young life, but many things are like a puzzle to me. I remember certain things like my first day of pre-school and being left behind by my cousin Candy. I don't remember my mother ever taking me to pre-school. I do remember I hated taking naps in pre-school. During nap time I was forced to lie down on a navy blue nylon cot. The lights would go out, and everyone had to be quiet.

One of the most important things I remember as a child was the songs the adults listened to when they got together to party at Jonquell Terrace, my first residence in Chicago, Illinois. The grownups had their glasses half-filled with light brown liquor. I heard Al Green songs all night long. Of course I was supposed to be in the bed, but I always found a way to peep through the door. I was curious and I noticed everything. Sometimes someone would come into the room to check on me and quickly yell "Get in the bed!" I had no choice but to listen to the music from the bed.

So many artists were played at the parties in those days: Anita Ward, Marvin Gaye, Al Green, Switch, Jeffrey Osborne, Menudo, The Debarges, The Isley Brothers, Tina Turner, Diana Ross, Lionel Richie, Michael Jackson and many more. My mother especially enjoyed the group Switch. To this day, one of my favorite songs is "I Call Your Name," most likely because I heard it so much and associated it with great times.

Mom and Me

Me in my Spider-Man Costume for Halloween

Back and Forth

Not only did music play a part in my early years, films did too. The movie *Friday the Thirteenth* comes to mind when I think about the early 1980's. I was terrified as I watched this movie with my godmother Marie one night. At the time, I lived with Marie, her two sons Brian and Roderick and her mother Maye, better known as Granny. We all resided on Estes Street in Chicago. I constantly lived back and forth with my mother and Marie.

My mother had four children by 1983. There was me (*1977)*, Odem (1979), Taleya (1981) and Jaron (1982). We all had different fathers. That was one thing about my mother. She had a weakness for men. If my mother cared about a man, she fell in love hard and fast. My siblings and I still joke about this today. She was determined to bring us into this world no matter the circumstance.

Chicago (Around1984-1985)

Around 1983 my mother and siblings lived in Baltimore, Maryland. I lived with Marie instead. I attended St. Jerome Catholic School in Chicago, Illinois with my older cousins Brian and Roderick. Our home on Estes Street was just a few blocks away from St. Jerome. While attending St. Jerome, every student wore the same baby blue polo shirt and navy blue pants. It was our school uniform and I didn't mind wearing the same uniform all the time. I was happy with whatever I had on. If anything, I was playful.

I loved to play so much, outside or inside, that I played to the point where I was held back another year and I did not advance to the first grade. I did not understand what learning was about although my mind took in details very well.

This was the first time in my life I felt ashamed. The day I found out I was going to stay in Kindergarten, I had to sit in my seat while my classmates took a visit to see their new teachers for the next year.

"Michael, you will have to stay with me for another year," my Kindergarten teacher said as I sat in my seat. Just like that, all of my friends were gone. I quickly got over it though and decided to play just as much as before since I had another year of kindergarten to go. I had some serious growing up to do.

When I think about what brought me joy in Chicago during 1984 I think back to the songs I listened to on the radio. I particularly took pleasure in listening to slow, old school rhythm and blues songs. I couldn't play any instruments, but I knew instantly if I enjoyed a certain song based on the melody. It took my imagination to different places. Music from the 1980's became the soundtrack of my childhood.

By 1984 I started to soak in the sounds of singing accompanied by instruments. I also reunited back with my mother and siblings. At the age of seven my life was like a roller coaster ride. There were ups, downs, twists, turns, high points and low points. It was a time of frustration and confusion. Just when I thought I was about to get off the dizzying ride, I'd be thrown around another turn.

Me in St. Jerome head shot

8

Me at the age of 7

Young Laura Layne

Who was Laura?

I loved my mom in spite of having to go long stretches without seeing her. She was a tall and thick-bodied woman with full lips that you could see a block away. Her smile warmed up the coldest places.

She was also bilingual, speaking fluent English and Spanish. No one would deny that she had a loving spirit. Her greatest quality was nurturing. Many late nights, I would wake up because my legs would be in serious pain. My legs would constantly cramp to the point where I could not walk. I always woke my mother up out of her deep sleep because she would rub my legs until the cramping stopped. Then, I would fall fast asleep.

Even though my mother was tired she always took the time to give me tender loving care. My mother was far from perfect but she was perfect to me. She was also very lenient with me. I don't remember getting into much trouble around her growing up. If I did exhaust her supply of patience, she gave me her motherly look. That "look" meant I was on thin ice and a butt-whoopin' would likely soon follow. I usually made sure to stay on her good side to avoid that look. Overall, Laura was a softy. She was patient, funny, kind, loving and very strong.

Mostly, my mother was a survivor. I felt like I inherited that trait from her. She needed all the survival skills she had. On August 18, 1984 my mother married my stepfather, Ellis. He was a new permanent father figure that entered my life. All six of us lived on Pratt Street in Chicago, Illinois in a one-bedroom apartment on the second floor. During my residence on Pratt Street, I attended Kilmore Elementary School, which was a few blocks away.

On weekends, I constantly went to a neighboring 7-11 convenience store to run errands for my mother. She always sent me to the store with a hand-written note in my hand to buy Keebler shortbread cookies and cigarettes. Because of my mother's patronage to this store, the hand-written note was all that I needed to get her cigarettes.

I wish I could call my life on Pratt Street one big happy time but this was often not the case. At the age of seven, if I had been asked to describe my stepfather I would've said he was Dr. Jekyl and Mr. Hyde. One moment he was a calm person teaching us how to read and spell big words. The next moment he was a monster physically and verbally abusing my mother. I hated to see her suffer from the slaps and beatings my stepfather gave. My siblings were too young to comprehend the severity of what was going on, but I perfectly understood.

One day my stepfather abused my mother so bad he later cried to me about it. He called me into the bathroom after the incident. There were tears in his eyes. "I'm sorry," he said. After he apologized for what he had done he said, "I love your mother, and I'm sorry I beat her."

I looked into his eyes and they were red from his sobbing. I stood there like a brick wall because I did not know what to say or do. He gave me a hug, but I was still confused.

As time went by, the same pattern of abuse continued. The hardest thing for me as a kid was seeing the abuse and feeling there was nothing I could do to help. The only thing I attempted was to tell the older members of my family what my mother was enduring.

My extended family constantly had a problem with my stepfather and his abusive ways. They confronted him, but my mother always found her way to go back to him. I did not understand this. At times we stayed with family members, but we always ended back with my stepfather after the dust settled. My mother said she loved my stepfather even after so much torment. She just did not know how to leave.

During this time, my mother had a job at a nursing home while my stepfather did construction work. Some of his employment was seasonal. He watched over us four kids without my mother's help on the days when he didn't have any work. He often became abusive with me. I believe it was because I was the oldest. There were times, I remember getting slapped in the face or punched in the chest, which knocked the wind out of me.

When he really got upset, he would put me in the closet for hours. I had to wait until my mother came home from work before I could come out of the closet. Seeing all of this, my mother never said anything to my stepfather. I saw the pain in her eyes, too. She always gave me a look that said, "I'm sorry, but I don't know what to do."

She knew what my stepfather did was wrong, but she wanted to avoid further abuse herself. My mother was in some serious pain mentally and emotionally. She did not know where to turn.

My mom in her nursing clothes

Chicago (Around 1985-1986)

In 1985, my mother and stepfather started a trend of moving from one place to the next. I changed schools all the time. I remember attending Stephen F. Gale Community Academy, located on the north side of Chicago. As normal, Gale was another school that was blocks away from our apartment complex. It was also close to Howard Street, the main street where all the stores were located. From dry cleaners to bakeries and game rooms to convenient stores, Howard Street had it all.

Mike's Playlist between 1984-1986

1. "We are the World" by Quincy Jones
2. "What's Love Got to Do with It" by Tina Turner
3. "You Are my Lady" by Freddie Jackson
4. "Last Time I Made Love" by Jeffrey Osborne & Joyce Kennedy
5. "Crush on You/Make it Real" by The Jets
6. "Hello Stranger" by Carrie Lucas
7. "Rhythm of the Night" by The Debarges
8. "Against All Odds" by Phil Collins
9. "Do You Still Love Me" by Melis'a Morgan
10. "Your Precious Love" by Marvin Gaye and Tammy Terrell
11. "Purple Rain/When Doves Cry" by Prince
12. "Through the Fire" by Chaka Khan
13. "You Give Good Love" by Whitney Houston
14. "Secret Lovers" by Atlantic Starr
15. "Tender Love" by Force MD's
16. "Saturday Love" by Cherrelle

Chapter 3

Public Hiding Place

I watched many adults smoke marijuana growing up around Howard Street. My stepfather was one of those smokers. He was cool and calm after he smoked marijuana. He even showed me where he hid his stash on the street so no one could find it.

My stepfather's only command for me was, "Don't tell a soul where this is." He did not want to lose his stash. If this kept him cool, I was not going to tell anyone. These were some of the intimate times my stepfather and I shared. I never said a word back then.

During this time, my mother was pregnant with her fifth child. On April 6, 1986, my baby brother Ellis Junior was born. It was an exciting time for our family. But the storm only calmed momentarily before picking back up again. The fights between my mother and stepfather continued. This caused us to constantly get kicked out of different apartments. Nothing seemed stable. Every time we registered at a new school, we relocated soon after. I never kept close friends. As quickly as I made acquaintances it was time to leave them.

In Chicago alone we stayed in five different shelters and a few motels. Some shelters allowed both parents to stay together with their children while others only permitted mothers and children. In those instances, my stepfather had to find other places to sleep. On top of everything else, the abuse did not stop, and my mother started getting tired.

South Side Chicago 1986-1987

I knew my mother had enough when we stayed on the south side of Chicago in a battered women's shelter. We got a break from our stepfather and lived with mothers who were dealing with the same issues. All of the women were told not to reveal their whereabouts for safety purposes. The songs that we listened to often were "Lies" by Jonathan Butler and "Lean on Me" by Club Nouveau.

When my mother wasn't listening to music with me, she went to night school. While she was gone other women watched over us until my mother came back home each night. Things were finally going well for us. I met a good friend by the name of Corey. He was eleven and I was nine years old. We acted like brothers.

Corey and his mother, Barbara, were from Mississippi. The funny thing I remember about Corey was the lisp in his speech when he said the word Mississippi. It was like he had a heavy weight on his tongue when he spoke.

Corey and I were a source of entertainment. We made small runs to the local penny-candy store in the neighborhood for some of the mothers who had a sweet tooth. Corey and I benefited from our outings. We got small tips when our errands were complete.

The money went towards Vitner's chips, large sour pickles in a plastic bag, Charleston Chews, Pals bubble gum, and taffy chews. The candy was sweet like this time in my life. When I was high on sugar, I would often hear,

"Laura, your son is crazy," from the other mothers. I did wild and silly things.

Sometimes Corey and I flirted with mothers who were in their early twenties. Our hormones were developing so we chased the older ladies every chance we got. Unfortunately, all of the hugs and kisses were poured on Corey instead of me. Corey was a little bit more up to speed than I was when it came to the women.

You always heard "Dance for me Corey," from some the mothers. Corey would then do the WOP to an upbeat song. He could dance.

I really looked up to Corey, because he was like the older brother I never had. Whatever he did I tried to imitate, which usually got me into trouble with my mom. My mother would often say, "Michael, you follow Corey too much. Get it together or you will be in trouble," Corey was a young Pied Piper, and I danced along behind him to whatever tune he was played.

Above all, life was good on the south side of Chicago. My stepfather was not in the picture and things were peaceful. All my mother had to do was follow the rules, then we could stay as long as we needed. There was no fighting allowed. Women were required to be in by curfew and couldn't use drugs. The most important rule was that the location of the shelter needed to be kept confidential, even from outsiders and family members.

For the most part, everyone followed the regulations. The consequence of a broken policy was getting kicked out. When I saw families get asked to leave, especially families I'd grown close to, I got sad. It was hard to see people come and go, but I was growing more used to this lifestyle.

It was like a dance contest. The judge tapped the shoulders of those not dancing by the rules, and they had to leave the competition. The main difference was that this was a lot more serious than a game for a fake gold trophy.

One day it was my mother's shoulder that got tapped. She'd broken two rules. First, she disobeyed curfew by not coming home one night. The next morning, I remember looking through the window seeing my mother sitting on the curb crying. I was confused and frightened for my mom. With anger in my tone I asked a counselor, "Why won't you open the door to let my mom in?"

She replied, "We cannot let your mother in, because she has to be taught a lesson!"

I sat by the window staring. Barbara, Corey's mom, watched over me and my siblings. "It'll be alright," she said to me over and over while she rubbed my back. Finally they let my mother back into the shelter. But we were not out of the clear yet. The second rule she broke was that she told my stepfather where we resided. This put many mothers in potential danger. I stood nearby when the counselor walked up to my mother. "Laura, you have to go." My mother's eyes overflowed with tears. She didn't say a word. She knew she had made a terrible mistake and there was nothing she could do to fix it. We had to go.

As we were packing I asked my mother, "Why are you still seeing him?" Her simple reply was, "I still love him." When I heard these words, I was furious. There was going to be no more peace. I could not understand why my mother wanted to risk going back into an abusive situation.

While my mother was packing, Corey and I cried together. We knew we would probably never see each other again. I was losing a brother. Corey knew it too. He gave me a bear hug and would not let go. Tears filled his face and I remember his tears rolling down my neck. Our time was up.

Mike's Playlist living on the south side of Chicago

1. "Lies" by Jonathan Butler
2. "Lean on Me" by Club Nouveau.
3. "Husband" & "As We Lay" by Shirley Murdock
4. "Go On Without You" by Shirley Murdock
5. "We Don't Have to Take Our Clothes Off" by Jermaine Stewart
6. "Happy" by Surface
7. "Candy" by Cameo
8. "There's Nothing Better than Love" by Luther Vandross and Gregory Hines

Road to Milwaukee, Wisconsin around 1987

After the goodbye's, we were on our way to Milwaukee, Wisconsin. Prior to all of his, our sister Taleya was sent to live in Florida with her biological father. Therefore, it was just us four boys, my mom, and our stepfather Ellis Senior moving to Milwaukee, Wisconsin.

The cool thing about Wisconsin was that this was the first state outside of Illinois I had ever lived in. Milwaukee was a new beginning. The day we arrived in this new city, I remember smelling the scent of chocolate. There was a large factory located downtown. You could smell the sugary treat for blocks. The aroma constantly made my mouth water.

There were at least two shelters we resided in before we relocated to a stable residence, which was a duplex in a small neighborhood. We lived a few blocks from Jackson Park, which was not your ordinary park. It had a pool area for the summer days, but it also had a lagoon located in it. This is where I first learned how to fish. Fishing was so much fun every time I visited Jackson Park. It became very therapeutic for me.

I caught everything from catfish to bull frogs to crawfish and turtles. When it came to making friends, I was picky. I felt no one could top my best friend Corey back in Chicago. I met a boy in the neighborhood named Terry. I can't remember his last name, but I definitely remember his first name because the name Terry sounded like a girl's name to me.

Terry and I became close friends. He taught me how to catch worms at night so I could use them for fishing bait. Terry and I sometimes spent the whole night catching worms. We had jars full of dirt and worms in one hand and a flash light in the other. You would think catching worms was easy, but this was not the case. For some strange reason, when I tried to grab them from the ground at night they moved and disappeared like lightning. It took skill to catch worms at night. You had to be patient like a crouching tiger then quickly grab them out of the ground before they could go back into the hole.

While I occupied my time fishing and catching worms, my mother and stepfather were looking for a better place for us to live. We had to find a bigger home, because my mother was pregnant with her sixth child. On November 6, 1987, our family welcomed a baby girl named Faye.

I remember the day my mother came home from the hospital. She wore a large pink fluffy trench coat, holding my baby sister in her arms. We were living in our new house not too far from the original duplex we once lived in. Our house was built on the top of a hill. The whole block had homes built on this same hill.

Talk about a hike, when my mother got out of my stepfather's car, I worried about her falling with my baby sister in her arms. Milwaukee was cold during this time so the concrete stairs leading up the house was frozen. My mother looked tired. Her shoulders were hunched over as she continued walking up the steps gradually, making sure she was careful not to fall.

The entire family was excited about our baby sister. She was very small and beautiful with a light skin color. Only my sister Taleya missed out on the experience of seeing Faye because she was still residing in Florida. While my mother was recovering from giving birth, there was peace in our house. My stepfather worked hard to keep a roof over our heads, especially now that Faye was born. He focused more on his job, which meant less tension between him and my mother. The future was finally looking bright for our family.

A New Change

By the end of 1987, things started taking a turn for the worse again. My stepfather went back to his abusive ways. The family was on constant alert because we did not want to get him upset. I never knew what mood he would be in, especially at dinner. Each time he would grit his teeth and say "Laura" my mother would feel his wrath. The same cycle over and over.

Every time there was a problem, I enjoyed going to school to get away from my stepfather's madness. I had to catch the school bus each morning to get there. South 78th Street School was a good escape from the tension at home, but being there was a challenge, too. Some kids who were well off financially could sniff out those of us whose families lived on welfare.

I was made fun of constantly because of the shoes and clothes I wore. If you wore Pro Wings, you were an easy target in the classroom. Some of the bigger kids were bullies, but being at school was still better than being at home.

At South 78th Street School, the only thing I really worried about was the last day of school. The bullies threatened to beat up people they did not like after the final bell rang. You would hear the horror stories from prior years. Some students would go all out and fight because they did not have to worry about being suspended from school going into summer vacation.

I counted down the days before the end of this educational year, because I knew I was on that list to fight somebody or get jumped. As the days on the calendar were marked off, I was on my very best behavior around the bullies hoping they'd forget to pick on me.

If being on my best behavior didn't work, I had plan B in place. I mapped out the quickest route to get to the school bus each day when my final class finished. The last day of school was not going to catch me unprepared if I could help it. God was surely protecting me though I wasn't aware of it at the time. Unfortunately "The last day of school" at South 78th Street never came for me.

One night my stepfather and mother got into another fight. Ellis Senior hit my mother to the point where I erupted. I yelled out, "I'm going to call my family." I thought these words would be like a wet blanket thrown over a small fire.

Instead it only added fuel to the raging inferno. My stepfather slapped me and threw me against the wall. "Who are you going to call?" he asked. My help was hundreds of miles away in Chicago.

I felt the hand prints from my stepfather's hand on my face for hours that night. My mother did her best to keep my stepfather off me even though she was drained herself. For the first time, she got the police involved. Shortly after, my stepfather was taken to jail. It was this incident that caused my mother to decide to pick up and go.

Mike's Playlist in Milwaukee, Wisconsin

1. "I Wanna Be Your Man" by Roger and Zapp
2. "In the Mood" & "Rocky Steady" by The Whispers
3. "Jam Tonight" by Freddie Jackson
4. "Cassanova" by Levert
5. "Don't Make Me Wait for Love" by Kenny G and Lenny Williams
6. "Never Gonna Give You Up" by Rick Astley
7. "Love is Contagious" by Taja Sevelle
8. "Foolish Hearts" by Steve Perry
9. "Spend the Night" by The Isley Brothers
10. "U Got the Look" by Prince
11. "Push It" by Salt n Pepa
12. "I Need Love" & "I'm Bad" by LL Cool J
13. "Reservations for Two" by Dionne Warwick and Kashif
14. "Love Changes" by Kashif and Meli'sa Morgan
15. "I Live for Your Love" by Natalie Cole
16. "I Wanna Dance with Somebody" by Whitney Houston
17. "Head To Toe" by Lisa Lisa & Cult Jam
18. "Hello (Beloved)" by Angela Winbush and Ronald Isley

CHAPTER 4

ST. PAUL, MINNESOTA
BETWEEN 1988 TO 1989

One day, I remember boarding a Greyhound bus and my mother holding my baby sister Faye in her arms. I had no clue where we were going but it was clear we were leaving. We traveled through the night and the trip seemed forever. I remember a man getting up from his seat and telling the bus driver to let him off. It was dead into the night. Looking from the window, there was no place for him to go. *Where was this man going?* I was puzzled but just as quickly as this man got off the bus he disappeared into the darkness. I always wondered where he went.

When we finally reached our destination, we arrived in St. Paul, Minnesota. I don't know how my mother set it up, but in 1988 we ended up living in a place called the YWCA right in the heart of downtown St. Paul. It was a place for women and children only. From our view, you could see bridges crossing the Mississippi River.

We were surrounded by skylines that connected buildings to each other throughout downtown. I figured these skylines were built to make it easier for people to shop indoors during the cold Minnesota winters. At night, I thought about how beautiful the city looked. You could see the night life from other cities that were miles away. There was even a building next to ours that had a large number one sign on top of it. It flashed red each night. It was a sight to see.

YWCA Building

Building with the large number one sign on top of it

Around this same time, The Nintendo Entertainment Game System was starting to become popular. I must have begged my mother twice an hour for her to buy the Nintendo system. "I can't afford it," she would always tell me. I knew she could not afford it but I bugged her anyway thinking a miracle would happen. I only focused on how bad I wanted it, not on the fact that she was right. We were barely making it, and my entertainment was the least of her concerns.

At the YWCA, they had activities for moms like movie and game night, as well as programs to assist mothers to get back on their feet. As usual, we met new friends during our stay. My mother met a lady named Shirley who helped her find a place to live in the suburbs of Minnesota. We moved into a three bedroom, one and a half bathroom town home in White Bear Lake, Minnesota. It had an upstairs and downstairs, which was a lot of room for us.

We had a nice place. When it came to getting food, we had to walk quit a distance to the grocery store but overall, things were good again. We just had to adjust to White Bear Lake because we were the minority. As I got used to the suburbs, my interest in other genres of music like heavy metal and pop expanded as well. I learned words to the rocking melody of songs like "Sweet Child of Mine" by Guns n Roses.

My mother enrolled my brother Odem and me at Birch Lake Elementary school. This was our first experience going to a school with a small number of black students. The difference in races didn't cause much tension. We made a lot of cool friends that lived near our town home. My mother started allowing Odem to tag along with me everywhere I went. I hated having my brother with me all the time, but she was not going to let me go anywhere alone. Some of the kids in the neighborhood had a Nintendo, so Odem and I would frequently go visit our friends. Some of the parents were probably not happy when we came to visit all the time, but we did not care. Nintendo was too popular and we knew who had it. When we could not play Nintendo, my brother and I were somewhere trying to fish in nearby lakes.

My mother on the other hand did not have any social outlets in White Bear Lake. She had no friends nearby and no family to visit. She also couldn't spend money going out to social events. She had to hold on to every little dime she received from the state each month. My mother was lonely. I never realized this until she made contact with my stepfather again. Her contact with him went from long telephone conversations, to him eventually coming to live with us in White Bear Lake. It was obvious my mother could not be alone, and the only man my mother knew she was comfortable with was my stepfather. She could not let him go.

My stepfather lived with us for only a few months before Dr. Jekyl returned. It was only a matter of time before we had to relocate again. We moved from the town home in White Bear Lake to another battered women's shelter not too far from downtown St. Paul. The house we resided in looked like a regular home rather than a traditional shelter. My mother made friends with other moms and counselors there as normal. She became popular with everyone because she made people laugh with her jokes and warm nature.

Ellis Senior disappeared, and we did not know where he went. With him gone, we were at peace again. Many times I tried to convince my mother to stop trying to contact my stepfather. I was tired of the fighting and relocating. Nothing seemed stable when he came around. We never got to know places or people long enough to grow because we were constantly moving.

We were in a safe place. I wanted it to stay that way so we could just be kids. One of the counselors named Nancy loved my mother so much, she offered to take Odem and me on an ice fishing trip for a weekend in the northern part of Minnesota.

Nancy and her husband had a cabin located up north. They went fishing and camping each year with their children. Since we were in the middle of winter, we went ice fishing on one of Minnesota's lakes. I saw trucks and wooded homes parked right on top of frozen water. The lakes were so solid Nancy's husband had to use a chainsaw to cut through the ice to fish. He also had a wooden home over the hole he cut out from the icy lake.

On this fishing trip, I made sure I did not fall into the hole, since it was dark and big enough to swallow me. I knew if I fell in and went under, there was no coming back. While I managed to avoid the hole, I wasn't able to avoid frost bite. When the temperatures dropped my hands got really numb.

I could not feel them and I was in serious pain. Nancy's husband rushed me back to the cabin to warm my hands, but they were so cold it seemed like the heat just made matters worse. Finally, my hands were brought back to life. That was the last time I ever went ice fishing.

Stability

My mother was always up to something. She contacted the same woman named Shirley who helped us get a place in White Bear Lake. I am not even sure what transpired, but I remember my mother telling me we would be moving into our own home in another part of St. Paul. Shirley was the owner of this property. Shirley set it up where my mother could rent from her. Things were set. We finally moved into Shirley's vacant home on Fuller Street.

Our house was yellow and brown. It was a three level home with four bedrooms, one bathroom and a basement. We had a small, built-in front porch and an upstairs balcony extending from one of the rooms on the second floor. I was most excited about the fact that I had my own room.

The house was located in a populated area. There were a lot of kids, small candy shops, a barber shop, and several fast food restaurants nearby on University Street. When my mother went shopping for clothes or groceries, she would catch the bus to Midway. I was so thankful for Shirley because she took care of us. She gave us furniture, and she left me a radio. I had my music and we were finally on track once again.

If you lived on Fuller Street, you attended Como Elementary School. My mother enrolled me there for fourth grade. It was a long distance from where we resided. I had to catch the school bus every morning. At Como, I had a good friend named Ray. We constantly acted silly in the classroom and stayed in trouble. We only hung out at school because we lived far away from one another.

Our home on Fuller Street

My brother Odem and I made other friends that lived in our neighborhood. If I didn't pick up any bad dating habits prior to hanging out with these guys, I more than made up for it afterward. I started chasing girls around the neighborhood. I had a story for Ray every time I went back to school. We talked about girls and sex all the time. At eleven years old we had hormones that were always on full blast.

Mike's Playlist living in St. Paul to White Bear Lake

1. "Sign Your Name" and "Wishing Well" by Terence Trent D'arby
2. "Parents Just Don't Understand" by DJ Jazzy Jeff and The Fresh Prince
3. "Don't Worry be Happy" by Bobby McFerrin
4. "Just Got Paid" by Johnny Kemp
5. "Something Just Ain't Right" by Keith Sweat
6. "Right and a Wrong Way" by Keith Sweat
7. "Make It Last Forever" by Keith Sweat
8. "Sweet Child of Mine" by Guns n' Roses
9. "Kokomo" by The Beach Boys
10. "When the Children Cry" by White Lion
11. "Hands to Heaven" and "How Can I Fall" by Breathe
12. "Look Away" by Chicago
13. "Waiting on a Star to Fall" by Boy Meets Girl
14. "Red Red Wine" by UB40
15. "What's On Your Mind" by Information Society

Chapter 5

Stability 2

I grew up quickly as Bobby Brown's song "Don't Be Cruel" played from my television and radio in 1988. I was too young to work, so the only thing that kept a little change in my pocket was cashed-in aluminum cans I found in alley ways. All of my money went towards playing video games at a local 7-11 on University Street. When the funds ran out, I hung around my friends. We chased girls for the remainder of the day. By the summer of 1989, I was exposed to sex. I kept this secret from my mother, because I knew I would get in trouble for even sharing what I knew.

Even during these carefree days chasing girls and playing Nintendo without Ellis Senior around, life was good. When it came to music, I constantly listened to one of my favorite songs called "Congratulations" by Vesta. This song had very sad piano keys in the beginning of it that kept my attention. It was something about certain songs that took my mind places. "Congratulations" did it for me.

On Fuller Street, I started noticing a lot of people coming and going out of our home. Things were beginning to change, and I did not realize what was happening right away. Sometimes my mother left us in the house with complete strangers we called cousins, uncles, or aunts since we were around them so much. If the house was empty and my mother was out and about, I watched my siblings until my mother came home.

I also kept the house clean so my mother would later allow me to go outside and be with my friends. When it came to food, my mother left food stamps for me to buy bread and hotdogs. Once I learned to boil, we ate bread and hot dogs many nights while my mother went out. If there were no franks, we made syrup sandwiches out of the bread. I got creative by toasting some bread, then put butter and syrup on it to give it a French toast taste.

I made sure my siblings ate when my mother was gone. She said she had to go out and make money, because welfare did not provide enough for her to take care of us. One way I knew she made money was through selling her food stamps.

The same strangers we referred to as our family members continued to come around. They smoked out of crack pipes in our rooms or on the steps leading to our basement. These "family members" were getting high, making a sale, or getting some rest before the nightlife. I did not want to admit it to my friends, but our house quickly went from an innocent family home to a drug house.

People in the neighborhood also noticed the change. Sometimes people brought it to my attention and teased me about it, but I didn't admit the truth. Just when I thought the darkest clouds were over for my family, a storm came. My mother was not just selling drugs, but using them as well. I never saw her do anything besides smoke cigarettes, but in my heart I knew she was on drugs.

She continued the pattern of not coming home for days at a time. Sometimes when she returned to the house she wore the same clothes she had on days prior. I took a stand. I stopped letting people in our home when my mother was not there. Every time someone came to my house I told them my mother was gone, and they quickly left.

The hardest part for me was hearing my siblings constantly ask where our mother was. I had no answer for them and just tried to do the best I could to care for them in her absence. When she was home my siblings were happy to see her. I was always ready to leave to be with my friends. My mother slept a lot during the day, because the nightlife kept her up. This way of life became a routine for my family, and as usual, I quickly adjusted.

BOOM!

One night on Fuller Street, the storm in our lives got worse. I was at a friend's house down the street when I heard a loud boom. I ran outside and looked around the corner to see where all the commotion was coming from. It looked like the whole block was packed with police cars. They were right in front of my house. I waited down the street for a while, but I eventually walked home trying not be seen by people. I finally discovered that the loud noise I heard was the cops breaking down the back door of my house with a ram to get inside.

People were talking. It was no longer a secret that my home was a crack house. When I went inside, I saw my mother sitting on the couch with Ellis Junior and my baby sister Faye. Jaron and Odem were not around. I suddenly stopped after I took a better look at my mother. I was shocked to see her, because I thought the police had taken her away. She had a ghost-like look on her face, and quietly stated in a matter-of-fact tone that the house was raided for drugs. "Are you okay?" I asked even though she had a shocked look on her face.

She held Faye a little closer and said, "Yes," without looking in my direction. The house looked like a tornado hit it. There were clothes and furniture scattered all over the place. It was a gloomy feeling to know there were numerous officers in my house. After several days went by, it was confirmed that we were getting evicted from our home.

That was only one major problem. Around the same time, a woman came to our house to talk to my mother. She was a social worker representing the State of Minnesota. My mother learned that the state worker would take us to foster care. This would allow our mother to get some help. It seemed like the tornado not only turned the contents of our house inside out, but tore us from each other's arms as well.

Just like that, we were being separated from our mother. The state found a place not too far from Fuller Street where an older lady kept foster kids. When we entered into what I thought would be my home for no longer than a night or two, I asked my mother, "Where are you going?" She cupped my face in her hand and said, "Mommy is going to get some help." But there was no timeline on how long she would be gone.

I assumed that my mother would be back in a few days and things would go back to normal. But several days passed, and I had no communication with her or a way to reach her. I missed my mother and wondered, *Will I ever see her again?* I had so many questions in my head and no answers.

I was impatient, so I took matters into my own hands. I ran away from my foster home several times. I stayed out all day, because I believed I would run into my mother on the streets. The first place I always looked for my mother was on Fuller Street. I never had any luck finding her there.

Our house was sealed. There was a sign on the main door I could not read from the porch window, but it looked like a warning sign or an eviction notice. Our belongings were packed up in large black garbage bags on the front porch. The screen door was also locked so I could not get to our personal belongings.

I then realized that we would not be returning to Fuller Street. I started going to different spots where I thought I would find my mother. I had no luck. I stayed out all night with my friends in the neighborhood. The nightlife had everything. You name it, I saw it on the streets. There was prostitution, crack addicts, people selling drugs, and about everything else you could think of that goes on late at night. I witnessed some of these things before the drug raid so the after hour activities were nothing new to me.

I just made sure to stay out of trouble at night, so I could continue looking for my mother. I hoped I would run into her on the streets, but it never happened. My foster parent who was an elderly lady stated she did not have the energy to keep up with me. I stayed away from her home too long. This only made things worse. She wanted me out of her house. She told the social worker my siblings could stay with her since they were younger, but she wanted me gone.

I remembered the telephone number my godmother Marie had given me years ago. I asked my social worker if I could make contact with my family back in Chicago. I bet they didn't know what was going on with us in Minnesota.

Forced to leave the elderly lady's house, I told my siblings goodbye. Shortly afterward, I was off to a new foster home. I thought my latest location would be close by so I could visit my siblings, but I was wrong. I was transported far away from everything familiar.

I couldn't run anymore. If I decided to run again I knew I would get lost. So, I was forced to stay put. The living quarters I was placed in was divided into two separate homes. One home was for boys and one home for girls. I was around many kids my age and older.

Everything was monitored, even bedtime. The strict rules and guidelines were new to me. The only thing that brought me comfort during my stay was listening to the songs "Cherish" by Madonna, and "I'll Be Loving You" by New Kids on the Block. The uplifting words and sounds of these songs helped me get by mentally. As normal, my imagination ran wild. I had nowhere else to turn, so music and my imagination provided an escape.

I did not stay too long at my new location. The social worker contacted me. "Your mom Laura is still getting help," she told me as I held my breath, not wanting to miss a word. "She will remain there until she is better." I opened my mouth in shock. I thought my mother would've been fixed by now. The government employee saw my confusion and continued, "You will be going back to Chicago, Illinois to live with your family. I was able to make contact with your godmother and Marie assured me she would take care of you until your mother is in a better position."

My worries floated away when I heard the good news. I was so excited to know that I would soon be reunited with my siblings and back home in Chicago again. I assumed wrong. The woman paused for a moment then continued. "Your brother Ellis Junior and sister Faye will have to remain in Minnesota to be close to your mother while she remains in rehab. Their father Ellis Senior would also be close by, because he had all parental rights."

Mike's Playlist living on Fuller Street 1988-1989

1. "Superwoman" and "The Way You Love Me" by Karyn White
2. "Heaven Help Me" by Deon Estus and George Michael
3. "Dial My Heart" by The Boys
4. "Darling I" by Vanessa Williams
5. "Love Overboard" by Gladys Knight and the Pips
6. "Funky Cold Medina" by Tone Loc
7. "Me, Myself and I" by De La Soul
8. "Forever Your Girl" by Paula Abdul
9. "Busta Move" by Young MC
10. "Pop, Pop, Pop Goes my Mind" by Levert
11. "The Right Stuff" by New Kids on the Block
12. "Shower Me with Your Love" by Surface
13. "Self Destruction" by KRS 1 and all-star rap artists
14. "Joy and Pain" and "It Takes Two" by Rob Base and DJ E-Z Rock
15. "Turn This Mutha Out" by MC Hammer
16. "Turned Away" by Chuckii Booker

Back to Chicago between 1989 to 1990

My family in Chicago did not want to have any issues with Ellis Senior knowing he had parental rights to his children. They decided to take Odem, Jaron, and me in without Ellis Junior and Faye. Marie was also able to get custody of my sister Taleya who still lived in Florida with her father. I was sad I would not be seeing Ellis Junior and Faye for a while. At least my mother would remain close to them while she continued to get better. In my heart, I believed that Ellis

Junior and Faye would reunite with us again. Until then, it was time to move ahead into the future.

Odem, Jaron, and I arrived in Illinois in 1989. This was the first time I flew on a plane. My ears were in pain from the altitude, but I remained glued to the window seat. It was amazing to see how small things were from a bird's eye view, then how quickly things grew the closer we were to landing.

I could not wait to see my sister Taleya and my family. When we finally settled in, it was obvious we had a full house. There was Maye, Marie, her two sons Brian and Roderick, my three siblings and myself. We all lived on the second floor of a three story apartment building located on North Shore Drive on the north side of Chicago. We had other family members occupying another apartment beneath us in the building.

When we could no longer stay on North Shore Drive, we moved north to Seeley Street into a two-bedroom apartment. Things were tight in our apartment on Seeley Street but we were able to adjust. As time passed, my siblings and I got a surprise on Seeley Street. Our mother was able to leave rehab in Minnesota to come on a quick visit to see us. I do not remember what transpired between us on her stay, but just as quick as my mother came, she returned to Minnesota. I had thought our mother would come back to get us when she visited. This notion was far from the truth.

After her visit I got the bad news that our mother was going to be deported back to her birth country Panama. The grown-ups never told us the reason she was being deported. I started thinking about Ellis Junior and Faye. They were going to be left behind in Minnesota to live with their father Ellis Senior. As for Odem, Jaron, Taleya and me, Marie was now our official legal guardian.

I never knew the heavy load Marie took on when she decided to take us four kids into her home, but she accepted the responsibility. She registered us in schools, provided clothing, food and shelter. She also provided guidance and discipline. She was always about business and order.

Marie drove a two door Ford Mustang, and managed to get all of us around Chicago. When we had appointments either with a doctor or for school registration, she loaded all of us up in her gray car. We were constantly on the go. Every time I hear the songs "The Secret Garden" by Quincy Jones or "Been Around the World" by Lisa Stansfield, I think back to the days in the Ford Mustang.

CHAPTER 6

THE SET UP: BAILLY MIDDLE SCHOOL

During the summer of 1990, we all moved from Chicago, Illinois to Gary, Indiana. Both Granny and Marie took me to Bailly Middle School for my seventh grade pre-registration one early morning. During our brief orientation, the school's secretary handed us a pamphlet that showed us the different events and activities Bailly offered. When I previously lived in Illinois, Wisconsin, and Minnesota, I never participated in any team-related sports or activities. I was ready to try something new in Indiana.

I wanted to follow in the footsteps of my older cousins Brian, Roderick, and Alfonzo who all played basketball. So I immediately said I was going to be a basketball player like them. The school secretary let us know that basketball season did not start until late fall so there was no rush for me to try out for the team. My vision of being a basketball player like my older cousins had to wait to be fulfilled.

The sport I looked at next on the pamphlet was cross country. I thought it was a sport that would take me across the country, as in I would literally be flying on planes, traveling across the country. At the time, I didn't know it had anything to do with running.

You can better believe I was looking forward to doing some traveling after sacrificing a whole summer of being grounded. Before moving to the city of Gary from Chicago, I ran up the telephone bill to $600 one month. This was done by making numerous calls to 900 hotline numbers I saw on television and trying to reach old friends back in Minnesota. Marie was doing the best she could raising us with limited income. A six hundred dollar phone bill was not in her budget.

She immediately disconnected the phone because she could not pay the bill and told me I was grounded for the summer. This meant no friends, no watching television, and playing outside was off limits. Furthermore, my bed time was 7 p.m. each day. This was traumatic for me, seeing as though the sun was still shining bright outside when I had to go to bed.

My freedom was taken away, but at the age of twelve I learned some major lessons. The first one was stay out of jail. Being grounded at home felt like a prison sentence. Secondly, if I ever picked up a phone, I knew to *dial locally!*

I could not wait for the summer of 1990 to end so I could start my seventh grade year. School meant one thing to me . . . freedom. I wanted to get away. Cross country meant getting away to me. So during seventh grade pre-registration, Granny encouraged me to participate in Cross Country. She also thought the sport meant traveling across the country, too. She said it would be good experience for me to see the nation. So my mind was set. Cross Country it was!

My Introduction to Running

While my mind was made up on traveling, Marie was focused on the Gary school system. She embraced it because children could be paddled by teachers when they got in trouble. Some teachers took their authority to new levels by creating holes in their paddles to give their paddles an extra sting once it hit a student's butt. Paddling was right up Marie's alley of discipline. Her motto was, "You act up, and your butt is toast!"

I was getting ready for a new journey in Indiana. Seventh grade was a time of new faces, new rules, and best of all . . . my own locker. It was another beginning of my young life. Basketball was still in my fall plans but I could not wait to travel with the cross country team. I remember the moment when I heard the announcement on the intercom, "Cross country practice will be held after school in the gym." I was pumped! When school ended for the day, I hurried to the gym.

I met a clean cut short man by the name of Coach Young who had a smile like the Joker from *Batman*. My first question to Coach Young was, "What things do I need in order to travel?"

Coach Young looked at me with that comical smile on his face and said, "Cross country is a running sport." He gave me a break because he knew I did not know better. I was confused because I figured running was for track and field. I sat there and wondered, *What did cross country have to do with running*?

Coach Young asked me, "Can you run?"

I said, "Yes."

He told me to make sure I had running shoes, and that we had practice the next day. I remember that first day of training. We went outside and he gave us a short route in the neighborhood to run to. Our job was to run to a certain street and then come back to Bailly. I do not remember how many guys were running that day, but I wanted to beat everyone on the route and hurry back. My competitive spirit was developing right before my eyes.

I made it back to Coach Young in first place that day. He saw that I had a knack for running, but to me it was just running. I didn't consider it to be something that could change my life. Who would have thought running would eventually take me across the country one day? In the seventh grade I was not thinking that far ahead.

The Battle Begins

Beckman, Edison, Tolleston, Kennedy King and Pulaski were other middle schools in Gary we competed against in Cross Country. Individually, I only lost twice in my seventh grade year. Both times were to an eighth grader who ran for Beckman Middle School named Ben. Ben was tall, dark, and had a muscular build like a sprinter. He had a lot of experience running cross country.

He beat me in a dual meet: Bailly versus Beckman and in a city-wide cross country meet with all the Gary middle schools combined. I never got upset when I lost to Ben. To me, running was just something to do before the basketball season started.

I never realized the opportunities that were steadily brewing for me as a runner. Marie was constantly being approached by parents and coaches about my talent. I, on the other hand, was more focused on playing basketball.

Marie had other opinions on this matter. She became so impressed with my ability to run that she continued to tell me that basketball was not my sport. She said I was too short and she did not see basketball in my future. I told her I would soon grow taller because I had family members who were tall. She stated I did not inherit any tall genes from the family and I would remain short. We constantly disagreed on this issue.

I was thirteen years old, and I still had time for growth. All of my thoughts of growing tall stemmed from the story about Michael Jordan. If he grew tall and proved people wrong in the sport of basketball, I was going to do the same. I also envisioned myself as my favorite basketball player Kevin Johnson of the Phoenix Suns. He was six feet tall, like I soon hoped to be. I wanted to prove Marie wrong.

The Constant Battle

Basketball season finally started. I basically sat on the Bailly Basketball Team bench for my entire seventh grade year. I knew I had work to do to improve, so I planned to work hard in the summer of 1991. When spring of 1991 came, I was still in the seventh grade. I participated in track and field. This is where I learned that competing in track was much different than running cross country, though I was good at both sports.

By my eighth grade year, I was a citywide leader in middle school when it came to running distance races. Coach Young saw that I was versatile on the track so he even put me in the long jump event where I could win and score points for the team. I was starting to get noticed by Gary high schools. I was a natural competitor, but basketball still remained my main focus. I just had something to prove, especially to Marie.

Between my seventh and eighth grade years, Marie and I disagreed on three central issues: basketball, the high school I wanted to go to, and attending church. I never enjoyed going to church growing up. I literally dreaded Saturday nights because I knew my entire Sunday would be spent in church. I didn't feel God was relevant at all. I could not understand the importance of God at my young age.

Granny explained to me that we needed to give thanks to God for His many blessings, but this information failed to take root in my heart. I wanted to spend Sundays with my friends. Marie knew this and used it as an incentive to get me to see church in a new light. Her rule was, "You don't go to church . . . you don't go outside to play." She felt that if we could not give God the honor He deserved then our privileges of playing outside would be revoked. That was enough incentive for me. So church it was.

As for high school plans, someone by the name of Coach Benny continually fed Marie information about what high school I should consider attending after my eighth grade year. She was captured by the idea of West Side High mainly because of West Side's Gifted and Talented program.

Marie felt that running plus grades equaled more opportunities for me. But between the ages of thirteen and fourteen I wasn't trying to hear any of this. I wanted to attend Lew Wallace High School known as (EL-Dubb or The Dubb). If you attended Bailly Middle School, you were expected to attend Lew Wallace High. Almost all of my friends were getting ready to attend The Dubb, and that was my goal.

Unbeknownst to me, God had other plans. Marie was instrumental in carrying out those plans, too. She did not want me to attend Lew Wallace High mainly because she saw potential danger for my life. I was having trouble with a group of kids at Bailly Middle School and she did not want those problems transferring over to Lew Wallace High. Middle school had a smaller scale of kids to handle, but high school had a larger scale of kids Marie was not ready to deal with.

God used Marie to keep me out of harm's way. He knew what school I needed to attend that would help me excel in my studies and running. Needless to say, after much debate over this topic, I was West Side bound. I spent the entire summer of 1992 coming to terms with the reality that I would never attend Lew Wallace High.

8th Grade graduation held at Lew Wallace High School

Mike's Playlist Songs starting off in Gary, Indiana

1. "Motownphilly" by Boyz II Men
2. "In Your Eyes" by Shirley Murdock
3. "With You" by Tony Terry
4. "Promises" by Christopher Williams
5. "Tonight" by DJ Quick
6. "Try Again" by Glen Jones
7. "No Rhyme No Reason" by George Duke
8. "Someone to Hold" by Trey Lorenz
9. "Just Call My Name" by Alyson Williams

My First Summer Track Experience

Me in my Steel City Strider uniform

During the summer before my freshman year at West Side High, I ran summer track for the Amateur Athletic Union (AAU) representing the Steel City Striders. This was the same summer the 1992 Olympics were being held in Barcelona, Spain.

Summer track for AAU was a new experience for me, because I met a lot of new people all over Gary. More importantly, I also met current students who attended West Side High. They explained what West Side was like, which helped my mind think positively about my new school.

A runner by the name of Tone one of those students from West Side. He was light-skinned with hazel eyes. He had the body of a sprinter, but he was mainly a distance runner. He also had a little sister named Kim who just graduated from the eighth grade like me. I remember her very well, because she was a fast sprinter who ran for

Edison Middle School when I competed for Bailly. So there was some type of connection being that Tone had a little sister who was getting ready for high school, too. He shared stories about high school with me. Little did Tone and I know that God would also use him to help change my life one day.

Tone and I got to know each other better during summer, because it was filled with track meets every weekend. When it came to AAU summer track, some of the rival competitors from different schools in Gary competed together on the same AAU track team for the summer. Marie was my biggest supporter. She attended every meet and made sure I was ready to compete each weekend. I qualified for the AAU Junior Olympics in track and field scheduled to be held in Rochester, Minnesota, running in two events: the 1500m and the 4x800m relay.

When we (Steel City Striders) arrived in Rochester, Minnesota as a team, the atmosphere was magical. Everything was so organized it felt like we were in the real Olympic Games. We definitely weren't in Indiana anymore. We met runners from across the U.S. and the competition was stiff. There were kids from other parts of the country who were better than I was.

In the 1500m event I got crushed and in 4x800m relay event we finished dead last as a team. I learned then that I could not depend on talent alone to compete in the Junior Olympics. I had to work harder and put in more time to reach the next level of distance running. I may have been one of the best in Gary, Indiana but outside of Gary, I was just another runner. I told myself I would be well prepared for the next AAU Junior Olympics. And I then focused on my next challenge . . . High School!

Mike's Playlist Songs in the summer of 1992

1. "Scenario" by Tribe Called Quest
2. "I'm Still Waiting" by Jodeci
3. "La Schmoove" by Fu-Schnickens
4. "Give U My Heart" by Babyface & Toni Braxton
5. "Just My Luck" by Alyson Williams

CHAPTER 7

ENTERING COUGAR TERRITORY

The West Side Cross Country Team had pre-season training before the 1992-1993 school year started. This was a time to meet my new teammates and get familiar with West Side High. Besides Tone, I met other guys and girls who were runners from previous years. Included were also people participating for their first time like me, and some teammates I was familiar with from summer track.

The infamous Coach Benny, who was the catalyst of me not going to Lew Wallace High, was nowhere around. I later learned that Coach Benny was not going to be coaching West Side boys and girls cross country. Instead we had a woman coach. The guys on the team were all smiles when they talked about her too. Supposedly she was beautiful and she had spunk.

I'll never forget the first day I met Coach Williams better known as Coach Tiny. She had a thin frame and wore a burgundy sweat suit. I believe these were the same colors of her alma mater Texas Southern University.

She immediately grabbed my attention with her loud voice that could be heard above any crowd at the loudest race. Her energy was like a ball of fire.

Coach Tiny was very cool and so real! Her voice was full of confidence when she spoke. She had the gift of encouraging you if you were down. She wasn't only smiles though. If you made her upset, she would tell you exactly how she felt. When you were in trouble with Coach Tiny, it was a big deal.

Everyone was treated equally on her team. Coach Tiny had the biggest heart. She would give you the shirt off her back if you needed it. That was the kind of love she gave and taught us. I wanted to run my best for this woman.

She set the tone before each practice by encouraging us to pray together. We started with the Lord's Prayer then quoted two New King James scriptures from the Bible. The first scripture was Philippians 4:13, "I can do all things through Christ who strengthens me." The second verse was Proverbs 3:6, "In all thy ways, acknowledge Him, and He shall direct your paths."

Even though I did not know what these scriptures meant, I went along with everyone else, praying before practice. I still did not understand the importance of God. I was more concerned with memorizing the scriptures rather than understanding what the scriptures meant. Coach Tiny was God-fearing and she wanted us to remember where we got our gifts. She taught us that our gifts came from God. Little did I know she was just dropping seeds on my mind and heart about the goodness of God.

A Sad Moment (Keep a bookmark here)

Before the fall of 1992 could kick off, my good friend and teammate Tone and his family decided to move to Minnesota. It was a sad moment to see Tone and Kim go but God was up to something in many years to come.

High School Was Officially In Session

Every time I think about West Side High, I think about crossing my fingers and throwing up the signs that look like the letter "W." The hand gesture looks similar to the Star Trek hand sign. I may be a little off but I am just about sure we copied this hand gesture from the rap group called West Coast Connection consisting of Ice Cube, Mack 10, and WC (Dub C).

So there I was, a freshman at West Side High, better known as The Side. I was in Cougar territory and it was a nightmare. In my first few months at West Side I was nervous, lost, afraid, confused and overwhelmed! I felt like an ant in a jungle. Everything was fast. There were teenagers of every age all over the place.

When lunchtime came around, many of the students would meet outside, go home, or meet up in The Surge if they were not in the cafeteria. The Surge was an area in West Side that many students met to: eat, talk, joke, flirt, rap, cry, laugh, listen to music, dance and gossip. I barely knew people at The Side as a freshman so I rarely showed my face in The Surge. The only students I knew at West Side were some of the runners I met during AAU summer track and pre-season cross country practices. But overall, I was still a total wreck as a freshman.

One thing I can say, the song "Real Love," by Mary J. Blige was heavily played by many upper-classmen in the Surge Area of West Side. It had this upbeat tempo and everyone knew the chorus. *"Real Love . . . I'm searching for a real love, someone to set my heart free. Real Love . . . IIII'mmm . . . searching for a real love."*

In terms of education, all of my teachers were serious about teaching and they made sure we were focused on learning. Their expectations were very high, and I did not want to fail.

I took normal freshman classes like English, Algebra, Spanish, government, science, and gym. Freshman English with Miss Williams scared me the most. Miss Williams was a firm woman with a deep and intimidating voice. She was a very strong and educated woman. Miss Williams simply did not allow excuses in her classroom. She would share some of her personal testimonies one moment and discipline you if you did not do what she asked the next.

When you entered her class and did not have your work assignments together, you were destined for embarrassment. She expected excellence and she demanded respect. You could not play games in her classroom. When you did what she asked, she had a firm way of praising you. I tried very hard to stay on Miss Williams' good side to avoid getting embarrassed. Every time I left her classroom, I would breathe a sigh of relief and be pleased that I'd made it another day.

I constantly looked forward to going to cross country practices after school was over. I could not wait to be around the vibrant Coach Tiny. She always kept things lively for us. Her voice alone made me look forward to the upcoming cross country schedule. I was ready to compete and kick off my freshman season.

Low and behold, I also had freshman basketball in my plans, but as usual I had to wait until late fall to try out for the freshman team. Marie was not excited about my ideas. She knew she was going to have another fight on her hands with this basketball dream of mine.

Freshman Season Cross Country

To my surprise, I had a very successful year in cross country as a freshman. It was amazing to run on all the different types of courses at different cross country meets.

53

I performed well at each of them, too. When it came to tournament time, our boy's team made it as far as the Regional championships. However, we did not make the Semi-State round, which was the race before the Indiana State Cross Country Championships.

Individually, I made it to the Semi-State race held at Culver Military Academy located in Culver, Indiana in the fall 1992. Sadly, I didn't make it out of the Semi-State round as a freshman so my first season ended at Semi-State. But my family, Coach Tiny, and Coach Benny were all proud of me for what I did accomplish. I considered the Semi-State race as a learning experience and planned to work harder for the next season. My mind was now set on freshman basketball.

The Boiling Point

This dream I had of becoming a basketball player was a nagging pain to Marie. She did not see basketball in my future. I continued to force the issue. I couldn't let my dream go. Now that cross country season was over, I looked forward to freshman basketball after school.

Marie made it tough for me to try out for the team though. During cross country season she made sure I had transportation home from practices after school. Now that basketball was in season, I had to find my own way home. It was at least eight miles from West Side High to my home in Glen Park. To me, it seemed like one-hundred miles apart.

When I did find a way to get home from freshman basketball tryouts, Marie gave me a curfew to be home by 7 p.m. every day. If I was a minute late getting to the house, I would get grounded. This meant no basketball. I thought, *During track or cross country seasons, I was punishment free.*

I could get away with anything. When it came to basketball season, I had to be perfect to avoid getting grounded. It was like walking on egg shells when it came to basketball.

I really started to get frustrated because I strived to make Marie proud by staying out of trouble and keeping my grades up. It seemed like no matter how hard I tried she never warmed up to my idea of playing basketball.

In the late fall of 1992, I was fifteen years old. I was maturing and starting to see things my way and my way only. I was growing tired of Marie's rules. Every time I turned around, I was in trouble for something. I felt her rules were only in place to keep me from playing basketball. Things were getting out of control, and the thought of running away from home entered my mind more and more.

The Last Straw

I had a good friend named Terrence (T-Gib) whom I also met during AAU summer track in 1992. He attended West Side with me and also lived in Glen Park. Terrence participated in wrestling, which was at the same time basketball season was in session. Terrence's mother, Miss Gib, gave us rides home when Terrence and I stayed after school for wrestling practice and freshman basketball try-outs.

One day, we were a few miles away from my home with the time showing 6:55 p.m. on the clock. It was like my thoughts took on a life of their own. They repeatedly shouted at me, "I gotta get home!" My heart was racing while I was sitting in the back seat of Miss Gib's Oldesmobile 88.

The time seemed to pick up all of a sudden and before I knew it, I was walking in my house after 7 p.m. I entered my home acting like I was on time. I immediately headed downstairs toward the basement as if nothing happened.

Before I could make it halfway down the steps I heard the words, "A You!" Marie called me and I quickly turned around and headed back up the stairs to go to her bedroom. My siblings and Granny were all in the same room watching a movie with her. Marie was sitting on her bed eating out of a glass bowl filled with popcorn.

I stood right in her doorway, just enough where she could see me. She immediately asked me two questions that I'll never forget.

"What time did I tell you to be home?"

I replied, "7:00 p.m."

She then asked, "What time is it now?"

I looked over at her clock with a smirk on my face and said, "It's 7:08!" My smirk made her upset, because the same glass bowl of popcorn she had in her hands was thrown at me. The bowl hit the edge of her doorway, just missing my face, and then it bounced on the floor.

When I realized what happened, I quickly ran toward the stairs that led to the basement. Behind me, I heard the commotion of Marie getting ready to come after me. I knew I was in major trouble. When I got to the basement, I did not go to my room. I hid behind one of the small couches we had in the basement. I peeked from the small couch, and I saw Marie come down the stairs with a broom in her hand. She immediately went into my room looking for me.

When I saw her enter my room, I moved away from the couch and ran back up the stairs to the dining room area. Granny stood in the dining room asking us to calm down. Marie was clearly not in the mood to relax as she came up the stairs after me. She was determined to hit me with the broom she had in her hand. She had to get around the dining room table to reach me, though.

Everything was out of control. My siblings were screaming, "Stop!"

I finally stopped running around the dining room table and said, "I dare you to hit me," as I was boldly walking toward Marie's direction.

I was fed up. My sister Taleya was holding Marie back from hitting me with the broom of course. Taleya cried out to me saying, *"Michael, No."* As I was inching my way around the table, I noticed I was several steps away from the exit door. I ran out of the house.

Before I knew it, I was halfway down the street when Marie finally made it to the door. She came outside stating, "Don't you bring your #$* back here anymore!" My life literally changed that night. I told myself I was never going back to that house again, and I meant it!

Up until this point in my childhood, I would say that my life was like a sprint. Typically, a runner stays in the same lane his entire race. In my adolescent sprint of life, I switched lanes constantly and sporadically based on the decisions and consequences of my mother and my stepfather. As I grew up, I changed lanes many times moving from Illinois, to Wisconsin, then on to Minnesota before finally moving back to Illinois. Walking out on Marie was the first time that I changed lanes on my own.

Chapter 8

On My Own

I was back on the streets. I did not know what I was going to do but I was positive I was not going back home. Unfortunately, I had the same clothes I had on during the day at school so I had to think fast. I quickly decided to go to my Cousin Candy's house.

She lived several blocks from my home on Connecticut Street. When I arrived at Candy's house, she took me in and questioned why I ran away. I told Candy, "I can't live at that house anymore." I felt Marie's rules were too rigid. I believed she did things in a vindictive way to keep me on lock down. I was already traumatized because of what she did to me in the summer of 1990, so I decided I would not go through that again. I'm thinking she would probably ground me for life if I went back home.

My cousin Candy told me, "You need to go back home when things calmed down. You should apologize for what you did." But my mind was made up. I would never go back to live with Marie again. Candy knew I was serious about not going home so she allowed me to stay with her and her family. I knew I put my cousin in a tough situation. She had her own household to take care of and did not expect to be taking care of a high school student. She also did not want to have any problems with Marie.

Marie eventually called Candy telling her she should not have taken me into her home. Later, Marie placed all of my clothes in a box and had them delivered to me. It was official, there was no going back. I was completely on my own.

My First High School Track Season 1992-1993

After I'd lived with Candy's family a few months, my first high school track season was getting ready to start. I was really looking forward to running again after a long fall and winter break. I knew I was overstaying my welcome at Candy's. I constantly got into arguments with her oldest daughter, and it was putting a strain on my cousin. Candy kept encouraging me to make up with Marie and move back home. She wanted me out, but I was not going back.

It's hard to believe that even with all that was happening I still kept school and running a priority. Trying to play basketball was no longer a significant thing for me. Life was starting to be more challenging. I decided to just stick with running because things were unstable in my life. Competing gave me a portion of peace I desperately needed. At the age of fifteen, it would be a long time before I understood what God was up to and how He always had His hand on me.

On my first day of track practice, I entered a room full of athletes who ran sprints, did field events and ran long-distance events. I was under the new guidance of Coach Johnson who was the head track and field coach. Coach Johnson had a trimmed beard, a dark complexion, and a shiny bald head like Mr. Clean. He was there when West Side High first opened its doors.

While I was used to Coach Tiny's energetic and outspoken personality during cross country season, I had to now face Coach Johnson's reserved nature in track and field. He was calm, quiet, and had an old school style of coaching. To sum it up, Coach Johnson showed tough love and there was no babysitting going on.

On the walls in The Surge, I noticed several pictures of Coach Johnson being involved in many track and field endeavors for West Side. In some of the photos, Coach Johnson even had hair! There were also pictures of past athletes who represented West Side High who were champions. One day I wanted to be there, too.

Well, each day before track practice, we would meet in Coach Johnson's classroom to go over future track meets and different strategies planned for the upcoming season. Our track practices were held in the hallways of West Side after school during the winter months.

As a freshman distance runner, I had a lot to prove. West Side was known for sprinting and field events but lacked strong distance running. That was my motivation to try to take West Side distance running to another level. I became wiser about running after my first taste of cross country in the fall so I was looking forward to seeing how far I would get in track.

In later years, finally making "The Surge Wall of Fame"

Regional's Tournament Spring 1993

"There will be a two command start. You will have a two turn stagger then you will break through the cones." These were the words I remember the track official stating to me and other runners before we started the 800m race at the Indiana Northwest Regional Track and Field Meet in Gary, Indiana at Roosevelt High School in 1993. The end of my freshman track season was on the line. I remember telling myself over and over, "If I just finish in the top three, this will be my first trip to the state championships."

I heard many great stories about the state meet in Indianapolis from the upper classmen. I heard about runners from Gary who were incredible in the past, and the trouble people caused during the trip to Indianapolis. I was also told how the team would be sleeping overnight in hotels, and how all the pretty girls from other high schools would be in attendance at the state meet. The state championship had it all, and I wanted to be there to experience it. The only thing I had to do was finish in third place, and my ticket to state would be punched.

I was a fifteen year old one hundred twenty pound little freshman representing West Side High in the 800m event. I was full of adrenaline. My heart was pumping so fast, I could see my tank-top jersey jumping up and down on my chest. My feet were placed two steps from the starting line. I was looking all around me and taking in every detail. It looked like the track became smaller with the number of runners getting ready to compete.

The stands were filled to capacity with friends and family. Everyone was excited to see the 800m race. The officials were setting up their starting guns and resetting the time clock. The sky was dark and you could see the school buses and cars in the parking lot directly from the track. The stadium lights were shining extra bright like they would for a Friday night football game. The stadium clock on the football score board continued to show lighted zeros.

The track official blew his whistle to let everyone know it was time to start the 800m event. Every runner was in their position on the track. The official stood at the top of the track so he could see all runners in place. He raised the starting gun in his hand and yelled, "On your marks."

I ran up to the starting line and my body quickly paused. "Pow!" The official's gun went off, and I shot forward like an arrow heading straight for a bulls eye. I stayed in my lane until I could see the cones coming off the second turn. I broke through the cones and I was well on my way past the first 300m mark of the race.

The race was getting faster by the second. Before I came through the first lap of the two lap race, I could hear the crowd in the stands yelling and screaming. The noise added fuel to my fire.

I could see the clock ticking away second after second. My first lap was fast. I was well under fifty four seconds on the first lap. "Just one more lap to go," I kept telling myself. I was pumping my arms and losing breath all at the same time. I was in a good position to go to state.

I continued to hear the crowd screaming. I really heard Coach Benny in the background yelling, "Mooove! It's time to go now, Layne! Let's mooove!" I could see bodies of people cheering down the backstretch but I could not see faces. Everything was a blur. As I was coming off the final turn of the 800m, I was still in good position to make it to the state championships. The crowd was screaming extremely loud at this point of the race as I was continuing to pump hard.

My body was in so much oxygen debt and pain. I'd never felt this type of agony before. "Come on! Keep pumping," I continued to tell myself. The crowd got louder and louder as the race was coming to an end. The finish line was in sight but not coming fast enough.

I instantly went from third to sixth place in a matter of seconds. Three other bodies ran right by me before I crossed the finish line. Just like that, my chances of going to the state championship as a freshman were gone. Not only was I disappointed, but I was also in serious pain when I crossed the line. I could not breathe. I think I held my breath the last 100m of the race.

I remember someone holding my body up saying, *"Good job because you ran a PR."* I ran a personal record of 1:59 in the full two lap race. I pushed my body to the next level and paid the price. I was still trying to catch my breath while taking in all the excitement. I got a lot of encouragement again from friends, teammates, and coaches after the race.

This was definitely a learning experience. In the end, Coach Johnson was very pleased with my performance and took me to the state championship even though I was not going to compete. He wanted me to get a feel for what state was all about. By doing this, Coach Johnson increased my desire to improve.

93-94 West Side Track Team

Changing Lanes

I could not wait to go back to Gary to start getting ready for the next year after watching the state championship. I knew I had a lot of work to do and I was ready. Around this same time, I was on thin ice living with Candy. She didn't want to tell me it was time to leave her home, but I got the hint over time.

I started planning to move out. Track season was now over and my first year of high school was coming to an end. It was time for me to find another place to live again. So I went to my high school guidance counselor and told her my situation. I too, told her I was not going back home to live with Marie.

My counselor helped me find a new home to live in when school officially ended. I was excited, because my new home allowed me to continue to attend West Side High so I did not have to transfer schools.

I was placed in a foster home not too far from Candy's house. I moved to Jefferson Street where I was welcomed by my new foster mom Miss Chris. She had a sense of humor that came off cold in the beginning, but she was a warm lady who loved God. I remember seeing a plaque on her wall with scripture saying, "As for me and my house, we will serve the Lord." Joshua 24:15

She said everyone had to attend church in her home. I thought going to church was behind me when I left Marie's house but apparently not. I still didn't know the power of prayer or the love that God had for me. It wasn't that I was opposed to God. It's just that at a young age church was boring to me.

I was comforted by the fact that Miss Chris had other teens in her home. There was Lance, another foster child who was a sophomore at Lew Wallace High and Miss Chris's biological sons, Evan and Eric, who attended Emerson. It was a visual and performing arts school. Miss Chris also had two daughters, Erica and Edra who were a lot older than we were.

All the boys in the house caused a lot of trouble living on Jefferson Street, including me. We constantly battled with Miss Chris on certain issues. She had to deal with everything you could think of when it came to us teenagers.

We all had raging hormones and we routinely debated and fought about everything.

Miss Chris truly endured, always keeping her composure with us. I learned around this time that my thirteen year old brother Odem decided to follow my path and run away from Marie, too. He was placed with me in the same foster home. I did not expect to start this trend for Odem, but the damage was done. I felt bad because Odem was too young to make a move like that but who was I to judge? I was young, too!

My Last AAU Summer Track Experience

In the summer of 1993, I chose to run summer track again, because I was on fire coming off a successful freshman year running cross country and track. Plus, I wanted to redeem myself from a horrible finish at the 1992 AAU Junior Olympics. I felt a lot stronger and more experienced. I decided to run for the Glen Park Ambassadors Track Club during the summer.

I was under the guidance of Coach Gardner and Coach Maybelle. I also had a good running coach and training partner who was from the island of Bermuda by the name of Coach Whaley. He had a strong running background and he was an encourager. I asked numerous questions and learned a lot from him. When it came to training, he challenged me on the track a lot.

As an added bonus to me, the Glen Park Ambassadors had a girl's track team. The girls were beautiful, but at summer track practice I could never really talk to them. Their coach wouldn't allow it. I had to sneak and make sure the girl's coach was not around if I wanted to flirt with the ladies. That was just me. As normal, summer track went by fast with all the races we had to compete in each weekend.

I qualified for the Junior Olympics in the 1500m again. The Junior Olympics was scheduled to be in Knoxville, Tennessee, and I was looking forward to traveling again.

Knoxville, Here We Come!

Every time I hear the song "Weak" by SWV, I always think about the long drive to Knoxville, Tennessee. We must have heard "Weak" about a hundred times on our way to Knoxville. Everyone knew the chorus, too. It went,

"I get so we weak in the knees I can hardly speak. I lose all control and something takes over of me. In a daze your loves so amazing. It's not a phase I want you to stay with me, by my side. I swallow my pride. Your love is so sweet. It knocks me right off my feet. I can't explain why your loving makes me weak."

When we finally arrived in Knoxville, I could feel the Olympic atmosphere as I did at the 1992 AAU Junior Olympics in Rochester, Minnesota. We were all eager to join the festivities and participate in the opening ceremonies at the University of Tennessee's football stadium. To save suspense, I made it to the finals in the 1500m in my age group, but I finished in the top eight spots. It was disappointing, but I knew I had more work to do. Overall, the summer of 1993 was a wonderful experience.

Mike's Playlist living on Jefferson Street

1. "One Last Cry" by Brian Mcknight
2. "Can't Get Enough" by El Debarge
3. "What's The Flava" by Young MC
4. "Think" by Patra

Chapter 9

Boys Will Be Boys

As the summer of 1993 was coming to a close, my sophomore year was around the corner. My foster brothers, Lance, Evan, Eric and my biological brother Odem were very close to each other. Lance was going to be a junior in high school, Evan and Odem were going to be freshmen, and Eric was going to be a sophomore. We were growing up fast.

The phone seemed to ring off the hook as girls constantly called the house for us. We constantly argued about who in the house had the highest number of girlfriends. Eric was the king but we did not want to admit it. We were always trying to outdo each other.

Sophomore Year 1993-1994

Sophomore year was a crash course in everything. Our West Side Cross Country Team did not make it through the rounds again. Individually, I made it through the rounds but I did not make it out of the Semi-State round. I failed like I did my freshman season.

Basketball was no longer on my agenda. I began to see that I did not have a future in the sport as Marie always said.

West Side had too many good players for the freshman, sophomore and varsity basketball teams.

When sophomore cross country season was over, I took a break from competition before the indoor track season started. This caused me to have more free time after school. I started enjoying just being a student with all the extra free time I had. I participated in many West Side festivities along with talking to more girls.

I was looking for a serious girlfriend, because I would see some of the male upperclassmen with their girlfriends by their lockers. Some couples even shared lockers with each other. I wanted that kind of companionship too!

Me in England sophomore year

Me touring England

Me competing in Hyde Park in London, England

Stepping Out

The first girlfriend I ever had in high school was a girl named Tina. I remember the night when I met her at a place called Celebration Station. She was gorgeous. We constantly made eye contact with each other that night, so I took a chance and approached her. I had nothing to lose because she did not attend West Side High. I did not have to worry about being embarrassed if she turned me down. To my surprise, Tina was also a sophomore at another high school. She was also interested in talking to me.

She gave me her phone and pager numbers that night. When I got home, I had a lot to brag about to Lance, Evan, Eric and Odem. I finally had a girl's phone number, meaning I was the man! My achievements didn't mean much to them, but to me, it was huge.

In and Out

Shortly after meeting Tina, it was official. Tina was my lady. But our relationship only lasted for two full weeks. All of a sudden, Tina was not interested in me anymore. She said I was too nice to her. She said she wanted a bad boy so our relationship couldn't last. My brothers did not let me live this down either. So that was always the flow of things on Jefferson Street. Everyone got talked about when something bad happened to one of us especially if it involved a girl.

Bible Church

On Saturday nights, we had fun just being teenagers. We stayed up all hours of the night but when Sunday mornings came, Miss Chris had a hard time getting us up for church. We usually found an excuse to sleep in or avoid church. I was sixteen years old in 1994, and I had my first job working at Walgreens. That gave me a valid excuse to skip church many Sunday mornings. If I was at church on Sunday, it was because I did not have to work.

Like Marie, Miss Chris believed if you could not attend church on Sundays, you could not do anything else. I will admit, on the Sundays I made it to church, service was great. Church started to become a battery charger for me, although I did not want to show it.

Other kids our age attended and worshiped God. I would not be caught praising Jesus Christ because I thought that was not cool. I was scared that if I did choose to praise Christ in the open, I would not hear the end of it from my brothers when I got home. I was under a lot of peer pressure.

At our age, praising God was not a masculine thing to do. We mainly saw girls worshipping but not us teenage boys. Although I did not praise Jesus in the open, I was definitely feeling something different on the inside. Gospel music was one way God touched my heart.

Before or after attending church, I always heard the songs "Speak to My Heart" by Donnie McClurkin, "The Reason Why We Sing," by Kirk Franklin, and "In My Name" performed by Kim McFarland on the radio.

These songs were in heavy rotation. They kept my spirits up. Each time I left church, I felt a sense of peace. I started to realize that maybe church was not so boring after all. I really started to wonder what it meant to be "saved." The word saved continued to come up in Miss Chris's home constantly.

Me working at Walgreens

1994 Indoor Track Season was here and Love was in the Air

When winter break came to an end, I was excited about the upcoming indoor track season. Getting to the state championship in the spring was my goal. I was completely confident I would have a successful year.

I remember seeing this cheerleader whom I couldn't keep my eyes off of. She was beautiful. She could dance, and she had a smile that was out of this world. I was too shy to approach her because she had a look on her face that intimidated me. Ultimately, my shyness went away. I was determined to meet this girl and get to know her name. So I asked another girl named Shaun, who was also a cheerleader, to give me her name.

Shaun told me that her friend's name was Sandra, but knowing her name was not enough for me. I had a serious crush on this girl so I sent Shaun to get some more information for me. Sandra sent Shaun right back to me. Shaun said Sandra wanted me to speak up for myself. Uh-oh! I had no idea what I was going to say to Sandra.

Eventually, I walked over to Sandra and confessed to sending her friend Shaun to her to do my dirty work. I smiled and immediately asked Sandra if she had a boyfriend. She instantly let me know that if she had a boyfriend she would not be having a conversation with me. I took her answer as an invitation to get her phone number. Although my brothers and I bragged about getting phone numbers from girls, the number I received from Sandra was special.

Sophomore Outdoor Track Season Was Here

Love and track & field were well on the way. As normal, our 1994 indoor track season ended at the Purdue Bomber Boiler Relay meet. This was the meet known to have some of the best high school runners in Indiana. The meet was also a preview of what the outdoor track season would bring.

When I started my outdoor track season, going to state was still my goal. I knew there would be major obstacles in my way. There were many other schools with solid runners on their team. But I was not going to let that stop me. My mind was set on the state meet.

I made sure to do the extra things outside of my regular training to try and stay on top. Sometimes when I attended Bible Church for the first service, I left church with Miss Chris's sister, Aunt Carol, to train on the sand dunes on Lake Michigan. Aunt Carol and her family lived very close to Lake Michigan. So I constantly ran to the lake to train.

It was hard running up the sandy hills and feeling the cold wind from the lake, but I wanted to get better. I was not going to let my chances of going to state get away this time. I made a vow that nothing was going to stand in my way of getting to the Indiana State Track and Field Championship in the spring of 1994. I always made sure my studies were in line to avoid being ineligible to run.

Learning from the Upperclassmen

By this time, I was making many friends all over West Side, especially on the boys and girls track and cross country teams. As usual, I really looked up to some of the guys who were upperclassmen, too. In doing this, I picked up some bad habits from them as well. I constantly chased the girls. The bad habits made me thirsty. But, through it all, I still had my focus on running.

Indiana High School State Track and Field Championship1994

Mission accomplished. By spring of 1994, I was on my way to the Indiana Track and Field State Championship in the 800m and the 4x400m relay events after the Northwest Indiana Regional meet.

I lined up Saturday morning in the first heat (race) of two 800m races at state. I finished first place in the first heat of the 800m with a time of 1:57. When the second heat of the 800m was over, the winning time was 1:54. I finished seventh place overall between both races combined.

The top nine places at the state meet were considered All-state. So I made it on the award podium standing in the seventh place spot. It was amazing to get a medal at my first state championship. The hard work in the fall and training on the sandy dunes of Lake Michigan paid off. I was hungry for more.

I could not wait to run on the 4x400m relay team. I had decent 400m foot speed, so I was honored to be on the team with three other guys known for speed. There were three total heats in the boy's 4x400m relay event. Our team was scheduled to compete in the second heat. As the race started, two of my teammates kept us within distance but we had some work to do.

We were far behind a lot of teams in the race. When I got the baton on the third leg, we were immediately in third place in the race. I thought this was strange considering we were far back in the pack. I held on to third place before I handed the baton off to our anchor leg, and we brought it home. We ended up placing third in the second heat but fifth place overall behind Lawrence Central, Evansville Bosse, Kokomo and Lew Wallace High. It was an amazing day.

Puppy Love of 1994

In the summer of 1994, I chose not to compete in AAU track anymore. I spent a lot of time running on my own through the streets of Gary in very hot conditions. I was focused more than ever on getting better, especially when I saw that hard work did pay off.

Junior year was right around the corner. I was looking for summer to be over with so I could get ready for my junior cross country season. I was fresh off the state championship in track and field so I was hungry to replicate that success in cross country.

Before the summer of 1994 came to an end, I went to the Glen Robinson summer basketball game that was held at the Gary General Convention Center. The game was crowded like a state level track meet. To my surprise, I ran into Sandra. She was dressed up, and had that same smile I was crazy about.

When I asked her why she was dressed up, she told me she came from a funeral of one of her good friends. Before I knew it, Sandra and I ended up in a deep conversation during the Glenn Robinson basketball game. I barely noticed the NBA stars present. I was focused on Sandra. So going into the 1994-1995 school year, I was determined to conquer two quests: making it to the state cross country championship in the fall and becoming Sandra's boyfriend.

Mike's Playlist of 1994

1. "Never Should've Let You Go" by Hi Five
2. "Long Way from Home" by Johnny Gill
3. "Think" by Patra
4. "Player's Anthem" (Remix) by Junior Mafia and Notorious B.I.G.

Class Was in Session 1994-1995

Once the school year started, I was finally comfortable with the fast pace of West Side High. School remained a priority in my life along with running. Our boy's West Side Cross Country Team had a successful year. We finally made it as far as the Semi-State championship as a team.

It was an exciting accomplishment for the city of Gary and West Side. We did not succeed as a team at Semi-State, but individually this was the first time I made it to the state cross country championship. I was proud that I would still be carrying the torch for West Side going into the state championship like I planned all summer.

I could not wait to run against all the top distance runners in Indiana. To much disappointment, I finished a horrible fifty seventh place at the state meet. I was determined to get back to the state meet my senior year. I was down but not out.

I still had the comfort of knowing I had someone to fall back on, and that was Sandra. By this time, we became real close. I'll never forget the first time I arrived at Sandra's house to meet her mom, Miss Cynthia. My nerves felt tight and twisted. When Sandra opened the door for me she had a frown on her face. It was clear something was wrong. She didn't wear that smile I was used to seeing. When I met Sandra's mom, she was upset about something. I wished I had not gone over there at that moment. But there was nowhere to run. I was in the hot seat. I had no choice but to introduce myself. Soon I learned that Miss Cynthia was cool and down to earth. She knew I had to like her daughter, since I'd traveled across town to see her.

When I told Miss Chris I was serious about Sandra, she told me to stay focused on my grades. Miss Chris said that I was going through my puppy love stages at the age of seventeen, and she did not want me to lose my focus. I agreed with Miss Chris that I needed to keep my grades up, but it was more than puppy love to me. I was crazy about this girl Sandra, mainly because of her smile. I wanted to see her a lot more when I had down time from training and school.

I Fell in Love with Her Voice: Faith Evans

I wanted to learn how to drive since I did not have someone to take me across town to see Sandra all the time. One particular day during my lessons, I remember hearing a woman's voice on the radio that instantly touched my heart. The voice was lovely and the piano keys and strings in this particular song were very different. I kept hearing the chorus repeating, *"Soon As I Get Home."*

I had no clue who sang this song, but I instantly fell in love with this voice. I eventually learned that the woman responsible for this voice was Faith Evans. I recognized her voice from the song "One More Chance" by the Notorious B.I.G. I eventually discovered that Faith was married to him, but that was all I knew about her. It was at that moment I had to hear more of her work. Faith's gift was heaven to my ears.

There was a record store on 45th and Broadway Street that sold music. I immediately went there to purchase Faith's single cassette for my walkman. I listened to the song "Soon As I Get Home" so many times that I'm surprised the tape didn't wear out.

I hoped that one day I'd get to meet her. I was drawn to her voice, but the name Faith was something unique. It was more than just a beautiful name. One day God would reveal to me the true meaning of faith.

Love and Track & Field

As Sandra and I continued to become close, I was so happy when Miss Chris allowed her to come over to our home on Jefferson Street to visit. For one thing, it was proof to Lance, Evan, Eric and Odem that I had a serious girlfriend. They teased me anyway, but it did not matter. My feelings for Sandra blocked all of their insults. When she came over she first met my brothers. Then we hung out the entire time listening to Faith Evans debut album I just bought on CD.

I had it made regarding Sandra and running. Things were moving smoothly throughout my junior track season. I made it back to the IHSAA Track and Field Championship in the spring of 1995. And I qualified in the 1600m, the 800m and the 4x400m relay. To my disappointment it was a disastrous day. I ended up performing poorly at the 1995 state meet in both the 1600m and 800m races. And our 4x400m relay team did not even place in the state meet. In spite of those outcomes, I believed I would redeem myself my senior year.

When the school year ended, Coach Johnson allowed me to compete at the National Scholastic High School Track Meet held in Raleigh-Durham, North Carolina to help me get some more experience. This meet was like the McDonald's All-American High School Basketball Game for high school track runners. There were top high school runners from all over the country at this meet.

Many of these runners were on their way to top collegiate track and field programs around the country. I was looking forward to the opportunity to run against these star athletes. I traveled to North Carolina alone. It was a scary feeling but I kept the knowledge of Coach Benny with me.

Coach Benny was always in the background helping me get prepared for races. He was a major supporter of me, not only as a runner, but also as a person. He was motivation enough for me because he knew more about running than I did. I trusted his experience. When I competed in the 800m at the national meet in 1995, I finished in twenty ninth place out of thirty two 800m competitors. It was another disaster, but it motivated me to want to return to this meet as a senior and do a lot better.

94-95 West Side Track Team

Junior year single pose

Chapter 10

The Finish Line of Senior Year
1995-1996

Senior year was here! Time seemed to run by faster than any race. I was finally at the top of the food chain as a senior. I was definitely no longer afraid to walk in the halls of West Side or The Surge.

There was so much to do my senior year. College was right around the corner, and I did not have a clue where I wanted to attend school. The blessing was that I had choices. Running opened many doors for me. I was getting letters from many colleges and universities around the country like: Georgetown, Duke, Florida, Illinois, Indiana, Purdue, South Carolina, Indiana State, Butler and many more. These were schools I read about in magazines or saw on television.

At the time, a Division One level track program was considered top notch, so I put all of my focus on attending a Division One program. I knew I would be competing amongst the best in the world on that level. Now, deciding on a school was my only challenge.

My last year as a West Side Cougar

Crash Course: Fasten Your Seatbelts

My senior year was a roller coaster ride. There were so many things on my mind including: my final cross country and track seasons, taking the SAT and ACT tests, my senior classes, prom, work, visiting and choosing a college, and simply going about my day to day activities being a senior.

I was only allowed five college visits per the NCAA recruiting rules my senior year, so I took full advantage of visiting all five. I planned to visit Purdue University, Butler University, the University of Louisville, the University of South Carolina, and the University of Illinois in Champagne-Urbana.

During my final cross country season, my ego got the best of me. My attitude got me kicked off the cross country team for a week. I basically disrespected Coach Tiny's authority and she told me it was time to go. Fortunately, Coach Johnson talked Coach Tiny into letting me back on the team.

I did some serious apologizing to Coach Tiny. I was thankful she gave me another chance. I knew my team needed my help and I worked too hard over the summer to throw my final season away. I put myself in check and Coach Tiny and I never had a problem with each other again.

1995 West Side Cross Country Team Gleason Park

More Problems

Just as things were getting better at West Side, things were falling apart at home living with Miss Chris. Senioritis was slightly kicking in, and oftentimes I arrived home late. I became a constant problem for Miss Chris. She noticed a change in me, and conflicts between us became more frequent. I began to sense there was a lot of favoritism in the house among my brothers. I stopped feeling like her child. I knew I was going to have to leave foster care after high school graduation anyway, so I started planning to move out before it was time to go.

Although there were so many distractions my senior year and life decisions I had to make, I kept my focus on my final cross country season. I had to succeed, because there was no coming back after my senior season. This was it!

The Final Season: Cross Country

Running in Hammond, Indiana picture
published by Hammond Times

I won every cross country race my senior season before tournament time. Then, I individually won all of the tournament races from Sectionals and Regional's at Lemon Lake to Semi-State on New Prairie High School's cross country course. I was well on my way to represent West

Side High at the 1995 Indiana State Cross Country Finals one last time in Indianapolis.

Before the big day, someone handed me the local newspaper. I held the thin paper up. It had a picture of me running, and it also listed me as one of the individual favorites to win the cross country state title. Say what? I was in total shock, because my main goal was just to make it back to state to redeem myself after finishing fifty seventh place my junior year. I mentally took myself out of the race before it even started, because I did not consider myself as a state champion. The nightmare of my junior state meet experience easily overshadowed the thoughts of me becoming a champion.

A runner from Gary by the name of Tony Williams who ran for Horace Mann High in the late 1980's, individually won the Indiana State Cross Country Championship. There is no confirmation if he was the first black runner to individually win a state cross country championship in Indiana, but the legacy of cross country running in Gary was already set before me. There was a small chance I could win state if I just believed.

There was so much hype going into the final week of the state meet. A doctor I didn't even know sponsored a bus ride for all my teammates to come watch me run in Indianapolis. My girlfriend Sandra, her mother Miss Cynthia, and many her friends also planned to be in attendance to watch me run. This was my final time to go out strong.

My former teammate Ed, current teammate Maurice, Coach Tiny, our driver Ronald, and I loaded up in a van the day before the championship. We were on our way to Indianapolis. On our way there, I constantly thought about how I wanted to run the race. I had some good and bad thoughts. I just did not want to fail again, especially with so many supporters coming to see me.

On race day just hours before the start, Coach Tiny gave me a lot of encouraging words. She told me that she was proud of me for overcoming so much and that she enjoyed being my coach. It was a very touching moment. Our relationship as teacher and student was about to come to an end. Coach Tiny did so much for me over the years. She was way more than a coach. She was a surrogate mother. It was time to do my best for her.

The attendance for the 1995 ISHAA Cross Country Championship was high. There were people from all over Indiana and beyond. The atmosphere was full of energy because the girls' race finished in dramatic fashion with a rivalry between two of the state's top girls going head to head. Everyone was anticipating the boys' race.

The Race

I was just minutes away from starting. I lined up at the starting line proudly, wearing West Side High across my chest. There were more than one hundred runners in this race. The stage was set. As I waited for the race to begin I continued moving, trying to stay warm. Just moments from the beginning, I got into position on the starting line.

All of the runners heard, "On your marks." With a loud bang, everyone took off. I immediately pushed hard to the front of the pack. The shouts from the crowd were a blur to my ear.

Through the race, I hung on to third place up until the 600m mark. When the race ended, I finished seventh place overall. I was disappointed at first, because I knew I could have done better, but I was still thankful. Just a year prior,

I finished fifty seventh place, and now I was seventh in the state.

It was a major accomplishment for me and West Side High. When my name was called to receive my seventh place medal on the stage, the West Side crowd went wild, shouting "West Side!" Although I did not live with Miss Chris any longer (I left her home on bad terms), I was very surprised and thankful she drove all the way to Indianapolis to watch me run.

My senior state meet in cross country was a moment I will never forget. It was like I won the race! Despite all the challenges, there I was finally on the stage with some of the best distance runners in the state. The perseverance and hard work over the years paid off. It was time to take this running thing to yet another level.

Finally making the state championship stage

The West Side Crew celebrating with me in Indianapolis

Coming home photo by Hammond Times

L-R: Maurice, Mrs. Hollingsworth, and Me

Mid-East All-Star Cross Country Championship (Kettering, OH)

Now that my cross country season was over for West Side High, I still had some cross country running left in me. After the state championships were over, I had the privilege of representing Indiana in the Mid-East All-Star Cross Country Championship. All of the top ten seniors from Indiana ran against the top 10 seniors from Michigan, Ohio, and Illinois. The meet was held in Kettering, Ohio and I finished an overall eighth place.

I was the first runner from Indiana to cross the finish line for our all-star team. I was surprised at this result, because I beat our state champion from Indiana along with four other seniors who beat me at the Indiana State Cross Country Championships just a week prior.

Mid-East All-Star Cross Country Team: Indiana

AAU Cross Country 1995 Joplin, MO

I still had more running in me, so I linked up with my rival competitor Jay Gunner from Highland High and other high school runners to compete in AAU Cross Country. The championship was held in Joplin, Missouri. I felt like nothing could stop me that day because I won the 1995 AAU National Cross Country Championship individually, and we also won nationals as a team from Indiana.

Finally, I competed at the Foot Locker Regional Cross Country Meet in Wisconsin. I finished an overall twelfth place and did not qualify for the National Footlocker Meet.

My senior cross country season for high school was finally over. I felt gratefulness to my rival competitor Jay Gunner and his family. They helped me get to these major meets. If it were not for them, I would not have experienced AAU or Footlocker cross country races my senior year.

Me at the 1995 Foot Locker Regional Cross Country Championship in Wisconsin

1995 AAU Cross Country Team (trials)

AAU Cross Country Championship in Joplin, MO

Me running at the AAU Cross Country Championship in
Joplin, MO

AAU Award ceremonies

Jay and Me in Joplin, MO

Transitions

Now that I was done with cross country season, I was looking for a permanent place to live. I was on my own again during the winter months. Miss Cynthia briefly allowed me to stay with her until I was able to find a residence. She knew I had no place to go. This allowed me to work out arrangements with my social worker on where I would live next.

My former teammate and good friend Ed asked his mother if I could live with them until it was time for me to go off to college. Ed's mother, Miss Debbie, instantly welcomed me into her home. I didn't know it at the time but God was really watching over me, because I had nowhere to turn.

One moment I was a top cross country runner representing the State of Indiana and the next moment I was looking for a place to live. Miss Debbie was another blessing sent from God to help keep me on the right path. There was something inside of me that would not allow me to make any bad decisions while I was on my own.

When I moved in with Miss Debbie and her family, I resided on Clark Road on the west side of Gary. Miss Debbie also had a full house including Ed's two other siblings Diane and Doug. I was very gracious she made room for me. Ed previously graduated from West Side in the spring of 1995, but Diane and Doug attended West Side with me. Miss Debbie drove us to school many mornings before she went to work. She took good care of me like I was her own child.

The Constant Fight

There I was, eighteen years old my senior year at The Side. Cross country was way behind me, and I was looking forward to a successful season in track. I used the 1995 Christmas break to train for my final indoor and outdoor tracks seasons. Snow and ice were everywhere.

When I went running, I always had to make sure I had solid footing because some of the roads were icy. The winter conditions did not stop me though. I was determined to finish my senior year strong. I knew if I just put in the work during the winter months, I would be in a good position by spring of 1996.

I put in so much time training that I didn't feel I needed to attend church on Sundays with Miss Debbie and her family. But this was a must in Miss Debbie's home, too. No matter where I lived, it seemed church was a priority. But I made up in my mind church was for perfect people. I was far from perfect so I knew I could not go into the house of the Lord to worship.

I did not want to worship God. I kept telling myself God had nothing to do with my life. Sundays to me meant sleeping in and eating good food. Praising God was not on my menu.

Miss Debbie had a fight on her hands when it came to me going to church. The rules in her home were simple. If I could not be thankful to God for His blessings, or follow the rules in her house, I had to go. Since I had no place else to go, I had no choice but to attend church on Sundays.

Trying to Decide

For some reason it was a struggle for me to worship God. I felt I called the shots on my life. Soon God would show me otherwise. Besides my struggles of attending church, I had to decide where I was going to attend college. There were numerous colleges scouting me my last year. All of my college visits were amazing. Each school was different and they all had many things to offer. I did not make a decision on which school I would attend right away. I felt I still had some time to decide where I wanted to go in the spring. My focus remained on finishing up my final indoor and outdoor track seasons.

Of course, there was nothing that changed in Coach Johnson's structure when it came to training. Every practice we sat in his Health and Safety classroom to get focused. It was his way of order and there was no way around his style. Sometimes I did not enjoy his routine. I felt that we could have finished many training sessions early if we did not meet in his classroom all the time.

But Coach Johnson wanted us to get our minds right and think about the upcoming season. Moving forward, I finished up the 1996 indoor track season winning a lot of races including the 1600m race at the Purdue Bomber Boiler Relays we consistently competed in every year before the outdoor season.

I was just one season away from finishing my high school career as a West Side Cougar. I seriously started considering attending the University of Illinois-Champaign Urbana or the University of Missouri. My chances of going to Illinois were very slim, because they already had a solid roster of runners. I never took a college visit to the University of Missouri so I continued to wait on what college I would attend. Nothing was official.

More Transitions

The 1996 outdoor track season took off. I gave Miss Debbie the hardest time. If senioritis was really a real disease, I would've been dead by now. I was starting a pattern of being rebellious and I knew I was eventually going to have to move again. On top of everything else, my girlfriend Sandra and I continued to have continuous arguments in our relationship. We constantly broke up and got back together. Our relationship was unhealthy. I started to have major trust issues. I stayed positive where track was concerned but my personal life was unstable.

95-96 West Side Track Team

Coach Tiny assisting Coach Johnson at the 1996 Roosevelt
High School Invitational

CHAPTER 11

CROWNED KING

My pattern of switching lanes in life continued. I relocated from Miss Debbie's home back to Glen Park and resided on Pennsylvania Street before the end of my senior track season. My new home was right around the corner from Marie's home on Connecticut Street where I originally ran away from in 1992.

On Pennsylvania Street I lived with my childhood friend Will and his mother Miss Price. Miss Price knew me from my early childhood days playing basketball with Will in the neighborhood while he and I attended Bailly Middle School. Miss Price was another blessing sent from God. She was cool, down to earth, loving and very understanding. She opened her home to me and told me she would help me if my plans were to attend college after high school graduation. I told her I was focused on going to college so she had no worries.

When I think back on my first days at West Side in 1992, I remember how traumatized I was just walking the halls of West Side as a freshman. I could not believe graduation day was slowly creeping up. There was still much to do before graduation. One of the most popular things was attending prom. Our prom date was scheduled for May 10th, 1996.

Before prom night came, there was so much hype about who would be crowned Prom King and Queen. You had to be nominated and voted on by your peers. I was surprised to know I was a candidate for Prom King. There were other well known students running for king and queen. I really didn't care if I won. I was just honored to be nominated. The only thing I had to worry about was a date. Sandra and I ended our relationship before Prom. So I asked my classmate Tisha Miller if she would go with me to Prom.

Prom night was held at Marquette Park Pavilion in Miller, Indiana. The theme was Candlelight and You. The song "Candlelight and You," by Chante Moore and Keith Washington was played periodically during the evening.

The girls were dressed in knee or floor length shimmering gowns. When it was time to announce the 1996 Prom King and Queen, Rose Cotton was crowned Prom Queen as my date and I looked on. When they began to announce the Prom King winner, I glanced around to see which tuxedo dressed classmate would get the crown.

"The 1996 Prom King is Michael Layne." I could not believe my name was called. I remember Tisha Miller giving me a kiss on the cheek while the camera lights were flashing. Wow! I barely knew anyone coming from Bailly Middle School and I never wanted to attend West Side High. Now four years later, I was accepting honors as West Side High's 1996 Prom King. It was a moment to remember.

After Prom, Tisha and I left Marquette Park Pavilion. I had to stop at a local gas station on Broadway Street. As I backed the rental car into position to get some gas I hit part of the pump. This caused the car to get a flat. It was a disaster and a quick ending to our Prom night. While people were enjoying the rest of their evening, Tisha and I were sitting and waiting at the gas station for her mother to come pick us up.

I was responsible for the rental car and blew it! The only reason Prom weekend didn't end terribly was due to the fact that Tisha and I enjoyed hanging out with our classmates at Navy Pier in Chicago, Illinois the next day. Because of my mistake the night before, Tisha and I carpooled to Navy Pier. The song I remember constantly playing on the radio during Prom weekend was "Let's Stay Together" by Eric Bene't. What a weekend!

Me as the 1996 West Side Prom King

Almost to the Finish Line

Now that Prom was over with, I was able to focus on track again. The 1996 IHSAA State Track and Field Championship were here. This was my final state meet in track. I made it to the championship in the 1600m and 800m events again. I was truly in redemption mode after my junior season.

In the 1600m, I placed in the top nine spots but my primary focus was on the 800m race. I had a big shot at winning the state title for the first time in my high school career in this event. When the gun went off in the 800m, I took off. I led the race until the last 150m. Suddenly Brett of Warren Central High ran past me and won the race. I was disappointed I finished second place, because it was my final chance to be a state champion.

Eventually, reality set in and I was thankful to beat my own record, running a personal best time of 1:53.88. The hard work over the summer paid off again and I felt redeemed. One week later, I finished second in the 800m again to Brett at the Midwest Meet of Champions. This track meet consisted of top seniors from Michigan, Ohio, Indiana and Illinois.

At this meet, I ran another personal best of 1:52. It was then that I realized I was getting faster as my season came to an end. I decided to represent West Side High one final time at the National Scholastic Track and Field Meet held in Raleigh-Durham, North Carolina. I wanted to see how fast I could really run against the best in the country.

Me in Indianapolis at the 1996 Midwest Meet of Champions

Pumping My Arms toward the Finish Line of High School

Before my last race, I had to get ready for high school graduation. Many seniors had their sights set on moving on with their lives. During graduation practice, I sat outside with a friend and classmate named Janelle in her car. The song by Kirk Franklin and The Family called, "Till We Meet Again," played through the speakers of her car.

I thought the words in this song were motivational but sad at the same time. To me the song meant that our high school days were coming to an end and it was time to go. But the song conveyed the message that even though we were going our separate ways, we would soon meet again. This song touched my heart, too.

Graduation day finally came on June 6, 1996. The auditorium was filled with people coming to support all the graduates. The stage was set for graduation ceremony, and I took in every moment. I could not believe my time at West Side High was coming to an end. Our Valedictorian and Salutatorian gave their speeches.

I will never forget Sharonda Grove, our Salutatorian, giving thanks and honor to God for allowing all of us seniors to get to this point in our lives. In her speech, Sharonda described different things she remembered about West Side, including my smile. I was shocked she mentioned me in her speech, but I was grateful that my smile is what many of my classmates would remember me by.

Ironically, there was a great deal of pain behind my smile that most people never knew about. I had to go through seeing my mother go through abuse at a young age then deal with her being deported back to Panama, constantly moving from one place to the next, and my siblings and I going our separate ways. Even though I caused it, I also dealt with the effects of rebelling against my birth family and running away from my home at the age of fifteen. I'd lived in many places throughout my high school years. But in spite of many setbacks, I had drive and endurance. Most of all, I had divine protection I would later discover in many years to come. For now, it was time to go.

When graduation ceremonies were over, everyone shared their last moments in the famous Surge. I took pictures with many classmates. I also soaked in the final moments at West Side High. To my surprise, my godmother Marie came to my graduation ceremony. She gave me a hug and told me she was very proud of me for graduating. I told her I planned to attend the University of Iowa in the fall since I was offered a track scholarship in the spring. Marie offered to take me to college after my summer break.

She also told me she took my brother Jaron and sister Taleya to Panama to live with my mother. I was excited for them, because they finally got to be with my mother Laura and learn Spanish. Shortly after Marie and I shared a brief moment in The Surge, we went our separate ways. For the remainder of the evening, I only wanted to hang out with Sandra. We became a couple again. We wanted to spend as much time together as possible, because I was going to spend the whole summer living in Atlanta, Georgia with Coach Benny.

Me on graduation day June 6, 1996

1996 and Beyond

Coach Benny had several things planned for me for the summer. He wanted me to work, save money for school, and to experience the 1996 Olympic trials that were going to be held in Atlanta. Most of all, he wanted me to train and get ready for college running.

Before I headed off to Atlanta, I had one more score to settle at the National Scholastic High School Track and Field Meet in Raleigh-Durham, North Carolina. My body was still in peak form so I had something to prove to myself. The money I received on graduation day from family and friends was used to purchase a one-way plane ticket to North Carolina. Coach Benny bought a ticket for me to head to Atlanta from North Carolina after the meet. During this time, I still resided with Miss Price and Will on Pennsylvania Street before I left for North Carolina.

My race in the 800m was scheduled on a Saturday and my scheduled date for departure from Gary was on a Friday. When I departed to Raleigh-Durham, the strangest thing happened to me. I got stranded in Norfolk, Virginia. I don't know how, and I'm not sure what happened, but I remember finding out I could not board any planes headed toward North Carolina. This was not the type of news I wanted to hear on a Friday before one of the biggest races of my life.

I was glad I still had some graduation money leftover, because I was able to buy a Greyhound bus ticket from Virginia to North Carolina. The National Scholastic Meet had races going on that Friday evening so I knew I would miss Friday's events if I took the bus to Raleigh-Durham. My only focus was getting to Raleigh-Durham in enough time to get some rest for Saturday.

As I rode the bus from Norfolk to Raleigh-Durham, it felt like the day would never end. I passed one mile marker after another as the sun gradually went down. I wondered, *Would I get enough rest the night before the race?* I did not want to repeat the same horrible finish I did in 1995 finishing twenty ninth place.

When I finally passed the last mile marker for my trip, I was in Raleigh-Durham. The only thing I could think of was getting off my legs for the next day. When Saturday came, I felt refreshed and ready to run. Coach Benny was not able to attend the meet, but he gave me some helpful preparation tips.

My personal best time of 1:52 in the 800m was good enough to get me in the fastest 800m heat of the day. If I finished in one of the top eight spots of the event, I would be considered a high school All-American. As usual, the stage was set. As I waited for the race to begin, the name that stood out to me was Michael from California. He'd previously won the mile race earlier that day, clocking a respectable time of 4:09.55. Michael was nationally known for his dominance in track. I was about to run against him and other top high school runners.

"Pow!" The gun blasted and everyone took off hard. One tall guy named Jason from Minnesota led everyone through the first lap. As we were finishing the second lap, I came off the final turn and tried to finish strong. My heart pumped fast and I tried to keep my mind focused. There were only four people ahead of me as we crossed the line. I looked at the scoreboard after the race and saw the winning time of 1:49.

I thought Michael from California won the race, but it was not so. The same tall guy, Jason from Minnesota who led the first lap of the race, won the event with a meet record time of 1:49.13. A few moments later the official results were in. I got fifth place with a time of 1:51.61.

Reedemed!

It was official. I ran the fastest time in my high school career and now held the fastest time in West Side High school history. On top of everything else, I was now a high school All-American. I did not expect to run a personal best that day, especially after a long day of traveling the day before. But everything worked out. I could not wait to tell Coach Benny the final results. He predicted I would run another 1:52 but I beat his expectation running 1:51.61. And just like that, my high school running career was finally over. It was time to move on and start my summer in Atlanta, Georgia.

Atlanta, Georgia 1996

I finally arrived in Atlanta in the summer of 1996. Coach Benny showed me a little of downtown Atlanta, but he resided about thirty miles away from Atlanta in Marietta, Georgia. Coach Benny was the manager of a local fast food restaurant during the day, and he coached a few runners who attended Life College in the evening. I finally got a chance to train with runners who were from the country Kenya during my stay in Marietta. Kenya was always known to produce many top middle distance and long distance runners.

Coach Benny routinely sent me articles about different runners from Morocco, Algeria and Kenya. I would always keep these articles to inspire me to work harder believing that one day I would become one of the best. When I had down time from training, I worked at a local Hardees restaurant, because they paid every week. I needed to make some quick money before school started in the fall. I also made a friend named Zane who worked with me at Hardees. He was young and very cool.

Zane was involved in music and did different talent shows in Georgia. Later on in life, Zane would become a famous rapper. I did not realize I was surrounded by so much musical talent in Atlanta, because I was more focused on training.

Zane and I hung out a few times trying to chase the girls in Atlanta, but a major part of my summer always consisted of training, working, listening to music, and watching movies. The movie I remember the most in the summer of 1996 was *Independence Day*, starring Will Smith. I spent my days listening to the album "New Beginning," by SWV on my walkman. Part of my summer went by quickly, but I learned a lot about college life living with Coach Benny. He gave me so much advice and words of wisdom. He was my mentor.

I enjoyed the experience of watching the 1996 Olympic trials held in downtown Atlanta. I was able to witness Michael Johnson break the world record in the 200m with a time of 19.66 at the trials. I met and saw several famous other athletes, too. The trials were amazing. I became more inspired after the trials and could not wait to compete on the collegiate level.

The sad part about leaving Atlanta was realizing this would be the last time Coach Benny would ever coach me as a runner. It is hard to believe he was the same guy who placed in my life during my early days as a runner when I was an eighth grader. Coach Benny was always there, either physically or in spirit. He helped change my life. Now I was headed off to a new coaching style at the University of Iowa.

The famous Coach Benny

Distance runner Bob Kennedy and Me

High Jumper Tisha Waller and Me

T. Williams 400m hurdler and Me

CHAPTER 12

THE FIRST MOMENTS AT THE UNIVERSITY OF IOWA

I was hours away from being an official college student at the University of Iowa. I daydreamed as I looked outside the window of Marie's rental van. Part of my family and I were on our way to Iowa City, Iowa. I was able to purchase my first portable compact disk player and spent the van ride listening to Faith Evans' first album over and over again.

I could not wait to become a part of the Iowa cross country/track teams, experience life living in a co-ed dorm, meet new friends, and see all the beautiful girls on campus. We finally pulled up to my dormitory named Hillcrest Hall. My room was located on the north end of the building on the first floor.

As my family and I started to unload my belongings from the van, they started to talk about how proud they were of me making it to college. My older cousins Brian and Roderick continued to give me that tough love speech about staying focused in school. I took their words to heart. I was sad my mother Laura could not witness my first moments of college. I knew she would have been proud.

The College Transition

Once I got settled, I was surprised to find out that Coach Ted was no longer going to be the head coach of the Iowa Track and Field Program anymore. But being used to sudden changes like this, I kept a positive attitude and looked forward to working with whoever the new head coach would be. I just wanted to succeed as a college runner.

The new head coach was Coach Wiz. He was the assistant head coach to Coach Ted years prior to my arrival. Coach Wiz was also the head coach of the Iowa men's cross country team. He was a former runner for the University of Iowa back in the 1960's, and he welcomed me to the Iowa program. Coach Wiz showed me around campus, and I remember him telling me that I had a lot of potential to become a successful collegiate runner. His words of encouragement made me more eager to represent the Hawkeyes. I was fired up!

I was amazed to see all of the athletes who represented the Iowa athletic program. My jaw dropped to the ground when I saw all the students on campus. I finally got the chance to meet my roommate Tim. He was from Waukesha, Wisconsin, and he was also a runner. I looked forward to rooming with him since we were both freshman getting ready to start off our college journey.

When classes finally started, I was nervous. College was a lot faster than high school. My first days at West Side High did not compare to my first days at Iowa. It was way more than I expected.

On the first day of classes, I felt like I was in a maze. There were buildings all over the place. I walked north, hopefully in the right direction. I kept a campus map in my hands to find my way to classes. In between classes, many students met on campus at the IMU. Many things took place at the IMU from eating, studying and taking a break between classes to buying books from the bookstore etc.

My partial track scholarship, financial aid and Pell grant were funds that allowed me to go to college. When all my classes, room and board, books and tuition were paid for, I had an estimated three hundred fifty dollars leftover to last me for a whole semester. College did not teach me how to budget money, but I quickly learned how to manage money with the remaining money I had for the semester. It taught me a major life lesson I still use today.

When I wasn't too busy studying my map to get to my classes, I often heard the phrase, "Go Hawks!" It was constantly shouted on campus. Every athlete knew what it meant. There was a lot of history and tradition being a Hawkeye. I could not wait for Cross Country, but after much conversation with Coach Wiz, we decided that I would not compete as a freshman in cross country.

Coach Wiz wanted me to train and adjust to college running first. Cross country training alone would get me ready for my first indoor and outdoor track seasons. So I trained with the cross country team all over campus and Iowa City. When it was time to take running to another level, we found our sanctuary at the Finkbine Golf Course.

Finkbine had everything we needed for solid cross country training. Most of all, it had hills that could get you in tip-top shape. I hated the hills but it helped me get stronger.

1996 Freshman Christmas and New Year's Break

My freshman fall training went very well. I learned a lot and I could tell I was a lot better. I could not wait to kick off the

1997 indoor track season. When finals were over, I officially had a semester of college under my belt. I was eager to get back home to Gary for the winter break in order to train and visit West Side High. I wanted to share my experiences with old teachers and disrupt a few classes.

Miss Price still allowed me to reside with her for the holiday break. She kept her home open to me while I attended college. I was very thankful. When I finally made it back to Gary for my holiday break, I continued training in the cold. I was in excellent shape from fall workouts so I did not want my physical fitness to fade.

When I wanted to do track workouts, I ran up to Merrillville High not too far from Miss Price. I would do track work-outs when the school was open. When the school was closed, I ran a lot of miles to maintain my base.

When I had some down time from training, I always caught up with old girlfriends. I could not go out to holiday parties or high school basketball holiday tournaments as much because I had no transportation. Most of my time was spent on the phone trying to catch up with friends or hanging out when I could. Sandra and I continued to date off and on, but our relationship was gradually fading away. She was now a senior at West Side, and I was a college freshman, so we were moving on with our lives and seeing other people.

I really did not date in college, because there were too many women on Iowa's campus. There were so many choices, and I knew I could not settle down with just one girl. This led to bad habits I embraced like running shirtless on Finkbine Golf Course. No secret, I truly had the three R's at the University of Iowa: reading, running and relations. I thought I had it made.

1997 Indoor Track Season (Cliff Note)

No matter how much fun I had on the weekends or school breaks, I made sure I was mentally and physically ready for running. The new year of 1997 came and Coach Wiz wanted the whole track team back a week early from the holiday break. He wanted the track team to get in some training together as a full team before we started the indoor season. It was back to business.

When I returned to Iowa in January, snow was everywhere. The dorms remained closed for the holiday break. Many of us competitors were placed in a hotel for the remainder of the final week before school started and the dorms re-opened.

Our first meet was in Minneapolis, at the University of Minnesota. The University of Iowa always competed against the University of Minnesota to kick off the indoor track season. It was crazy to return back to the Twin Cities after being there in 1989.

I thought about my younger siblings Ellis Junior and Faye. I often wondered how they were doing and if I would have a chance to run into them while I competed in Minnesota. I was their older brother and cared about them. At this point though, all I could do was hope they were doing okay since I had no way of finding them.

When we finally made it to Minneapolis to compete, it was cold. All the distance runners ran outside in the freezing temperatures just to warm up before our individual races. Enduring the elements was part of the life of a distance runner. We ran everywhere no matter the weather conditions.

Michael Layne

The 1997 Indoor Big 10 Conference Hosted by the University of Iowa

Every year the different schools in the Big 10 Conference would host many conference championships. The University of Iowa was on schedule to host the 1997 Indoor Big 10 Conference Track and Field Championship. Everyone in Iowa City was looking forward to this special event. For a few seniors, it was their last conference meet. For us new comers, it was just the beginning.

My indoor season was solid. I posted a 1:51.54 in the 800m event which was one of the fastest times in indoor Big 10 Conference in 1997. I ran this time on Iowa State's 300m indoor track. Even though I had a fast time going into the 1997 Indoor Big 10 Conference track meet, I remained humble. It was amazing to see that in less than one year, I was running times it took me all season to run in high school. I was getting stronger and I could not wait to see what I could do in the Big 10 Conference.

I called Miss Price to give her the good news and information. She instantly planned to take a trip to Iowa to watch me compete. She was also bringing a few of my friends from Gary to watch me run on championship weekend. There was so much excitement leading up to the Big 10 Conference meet.

A local reporter did a news article on me going into the championship. The story talked about my success as a runner and a small conflict that took place when I visited the University of Illinois while in high school.

The talk was that Illinois turned me away. I told the reporter the conflict was not a big issue for me, because I felt I represented one of the best schools in the country, and that was Iowa. The only thing I was focused on was doing my best in the conference championship in front of many Iowa fans and my friends.

Our track team had a full roster of competitors. Everyone on the team competing knew what they needed to do in their special events. My good friend and training partner Jimmy and I represented the Iowa Hawkeyes in the 800m event. We had a lot on our plates in the 800m, because the University of Illinois, Penn State University and the University of Michigan had tough competitors who ran the same event. It was show time!

Jimmy and I both qualified for Sunday's finals in the 800m event which meant we could score team points for Iowa on the final day of competition. As we lined up on the starting line for finals, the indoor stadium was packed. My heart continued to jump up and down as it did before every race.

I heard the words "On Your Marks!" I ran up to the line, quickly paused and then the gun went off. *Pow!* The crowd immediately starting cheering, "Go Hawks!" We had four laps to go on the 200m indoor track. Laps one and two went by easily and the race started to get faster.

I was sitting in the back of the race watching the runners battling for position as the race was gradually coming to an end. The bell lap went off going into the final lap and the crowd's cheering grew louder by the second. I finally moved from the back of the pack to get myself in position. Once I was in place, I started sprinting down the small back stretch to catch a few runners.

When I came off the final turn, I saw the clock winding down and four other runners in front of me crossing the finish line. The winner of the race was from Penn State. Jimmy and I came in fifth and sixth place helping the Iowa Hawkeyes finish fourth place overall as a team in the Indoor Big 10 Conference.

Me finishing 5th place at the
1997 Indoor Big 10's story by Daily Iowan

Freshman Year Story by Daily Iowan

1997 Outdoor Track Season

To kick off the 1997 outdoor track season, we traveled west on our spring break. It was my first time in California. Assistant Coach Pat knew the state very well from his competitive days. He took us around different cities in California when we had down time from training.

The song that instantly comes to my mind when I think about California is "Hypnotize" by Notorious B.I.G. This song constantly played on the radio while we toured different cities. Many people on the team looked forward to getting the latest Notorious B.I.G. album. I was a late bloomer when it came to grasping the true lyrics of the Notorious B.I.G., but I anticipated his album, too. For me, it was the old school beat in "Hypnotize" that made it lively.

In our continued down time from training, some of my teammates and I went to see the movie *Love Jones*. After we saw this movie, we came out of the theatres looking for love. We talked about how this movie triggered us to go look for that special someone. I couldn't wait to get back to Iowa.

The team was hilarious at times, too. We constantly joked and teased each other on van rides to meets or practice. You put a bunch of college guys together in a van and you are going to get nothing but laughter. It was some of the most memorable moments in my life. I was on a great team being exposed to so much. In return, I wanted to run my best for the University of Iowa.

Jimmy D. and Me in California at USC track meet 1997

1997 Drake Relays in Des Moines, Iowa

1997 University of Iowa Track Team

Fast Forward

My freshman year was gradually coming to an end with classes and competitions. I had a decent outdoor track season but not good enough to qualify for the NCAA Outdoor Track and Field Championship. The Big 10 Conference Outdoor Track and Field Championships were scheduled to be held at the University of Illinois Champaign-Urbana. I let Marie know that I would be competing in Illinois at the Big 10 Conference meet since it was closer to Gary, Indiana. She told me she would come to support me.

The 800m trials were underway at the University of Illinois Champaign-Urbana. The words I heard a million times, "On your Marks!" I braced myself for the upcoming run. The gun blasted and I took off. My family was in the stands cheering as I went by the first lap in the lead. I felt strong going into the second lap of the race. I held the lead going down the back stretch away from the 300m mark. I heard my coaches and teammates encouraging me to bring it home.

I knew Bobby from Illinois would be coming after me soon, so I stayed focused coming off the final turn to the finish line. Bobby came alongside me, and we both looked at each other. As he took the lead, we started looking around to make sure we were in good position to automatically qualify for the finals. Bobby and I finished one and two in our heat. We qualified and looked forward to the next day. I ran a time of 1:50 with ease in the trials. It was not the fastest time I ran during the season, but it was a major step forward for my confidence. I was not tired at all.

Coach Wiz quickly pulled me to the side and told me how strong I looked running past the 600m mark at 1:19 then coasting the rest of the way to the finish line. He stated, "You are ready for the finals tomorrow." I took his words to heart and quickly started getting mentally ready. I waved to my family that still remained in the stands to enjoy the rest of the Big 10 Conference meet. After the meet my family gave me many words of encouragement. Tomorrow was show time!

Bobby and Me in the 800m trials 1997
Outdoor Big 10's photo by Daily Illini

The End of my Freshman Collegiate Year (School and Track)

The next day I was ready to put on a show. I felt like the underdog going into the finals. I was confident I could pull off an upset claiming victory at the Big 10 championship with the way I ran the day before.

127

Pow! The 800m finals were underway! I quickly broke through the cones on the first turn of the race. The stadium was filled with spectators and all the runners in Big 10 Conference (both the men's and women's track teams) were present. The first lap went by fast. I heard "ting-a-ling-ling-ling-ling" . . . The bell lap.

Just one more lap to go. There was something about the bell lap that made all the runners step it up. Everyone in the 800m was getting into position coming off the third turn. I could see Bobby of Illinois moving in first position going down the back stretch and I was getting ready to set up my "final kick" to bring it home. The race was getting faster as everyone headed towards the 600m mark. It was time to go. Just 200m left . . . then it happened!

I got bumped out of position by a runner from Purdue University running into the final turn. I lost all momentum and drive in one of the most critical parts of the 800m race when I got bumped. When I came off the final turn it was too late! I could see everyone rushing toward the finish line as the crowd got louder. As I was approaching the finish line in last place, I could hear the crowd's sympathy claps.

I finished dead last in the finals. I was totally embarrassed that my family and teammates witnessed my setback. So much hard work was put into my freshman season, and it quickly ended with a bump. To make matters worse, the runner from Purdue University who bumped me finished second place. His final kick set him up in good position in the end.

This was what I was shooting for in the race. Deep down inside I knew I could have possibly snuck in a win or finished high but it was not meant to be. What could have been a defining moment in my running career turned into a failing seed planted in my mind, because I never finished last place in any race in my entire career until then.

My teammates and coaches gave me support after they witnessed my fall. Coach Wiz told me to pick my head up and take in moments like this, because I was just a freshman. He told me I had accomplished a lot and that I had a lot to look forward to in years to come.

I must've had a million what ifs and play backs in my mind after that race. I could not let it go, because I knew I worked hard starting in the fall of 1996. I expected to do some great things my freshman year. But instead it was back to the drawing board for next season.

The Giant Leap

Freshman year was history. I viewed it as successful, because I learned so much when it came to running, and I made it through all of my classes. I no longer dreaded going to college, wondering if I would make it as a student. I remained in Iowa City for the summer of 1997 to train and take a summer class to free up a little of my schedule during the fall.

The dorms were closed for the summer break, so I lived with some of my teammates in an apartment. Our place of residence was located just a few blocks away from Carver Hawkeye Arena. It was a hot summer in more ways than one.

The summer of 1997 consisted of classes, working with the youth leadership summer program, training, and chasing the girls that lived in and around Iowa City. My priorities were in place when it came to school and training, but I was far from innocent while on summer break.

When the summer gradually came to a close, I moved my things back to Hillcrest Hall dormitory. Tim and I became very close as roommates our freshman year so we decided to partner-up again. We also added a new roommate sophomore year. Kevin was a 400m sprinter on the track team so it was a smooth transition for all of us to live together. We were student athletes and we knew what it took when it came to sacrificing.

I was ready for my first cross country season in the fall of 1997. I knew cross country would be the foundation of a successful track season so I looked forward to competing and taking my training to another level. Coach Wiz wanted us to get into the habit of using our time wisely as runners. We would meet up at the Old Capital building on campus many mornings as a team to get in short runs before classes.

Being a distance runner, we had to eat, sleep and dream running. There was no time to take a day off if you were trying to get to the next level. We constantly ran all over Iowa City and beyond many Sundays, too. It was a true sacrifice.

CHAPTER 13

THE UNIVERSITY OF IOWA'S NCAA CROSS COUNTRY TEAM APPEARANCE (FALL 1998)

The sacrifices the cross country team made paid off. The University of Iowa made it as a group to run in the 1998 NCAA Cross Country Championship held in Kansas. This was Coach Wiz's first appearance having a full team compete on the national stage. It was a major accomplishment for all of us and we were looking forward to running against national powerhouses like Arkansas, Stanford, Michigan, Wisconsin and other great schools across the country.

Coach Wiz even set up a time for the whole team to meet a well-known, world wrestler by the name of Mr. Dan Gee. He was the head coach for the Iowa wrestling team, and we all respected him because of his history and his tough mentality. We took in his positive advice before competing in one of the biggest races of our lives.

So there we were, lined up at the Division I and II 1998 NCAA Cross Country Championship in Lawrence, Kansas. The host sight was Rim Rock Farm. The women had just finished their race and everyone was getting ready to watch the men's race. The field was packed with the best runners from all parts of the country and the world. The men had to run a 10k, a grueling six plus miles on hilly terrain, but everyone on the team was up to the task.

The race got off to a fast start. The lead runners took off, and I never saw them again. Just when I thought I was in a good position, I got lost in the crowd of more than two hundred runners. I felt like I was in a runner's nightmare. I was way in the back of several packs.

The race felt like a marathon. Finally, I got to the end of the race. It was only then that I saw the top runners who'd already finished. I knew it was not my best performance. As a team, we finished in the top twenty five among all the schools. I knew individually I let my team down, so I continued to look forward to the upcoming indoor and outdoor track seasons. That seemed to become a pattern. All of my current seasons seemed like a rebound for the next season.

1998 NCAA Cross Country Championship in Kansas

Iowa Cross Country Team

Individual Cross Country photo of Me

Seneca and Me at the 1998
NCAA Cross Country Championship

Senior Year

It was now my senior year, but I didn't feel like celebrating. I felt like I was running backwards. I started questioning myself and my training, because there were no major breakthroughs. I expected to be one of the top runners in the country by my senior year, but instead I was still running times I ran my freshman year in college. I was not getting any better.

A million questions crossed my mind constantly. *Did more running mean better? Did less running and more quality training mean better?* My mind had so many doubts and disappointments I ended up meeting with a sports psychologist. My running career hit a metaphorical hurdle that I couldn't jump over. *How do I move forward?* Going into the fall of 1999, I decided not to compete in Cross Country anymore. Part of my decision was tactical.

I wanted to take the same approach I did as a freshman and just focus on training. My goal was to restore my mind from competing and get ready for the upcoming indoor and outdoor track seasons in the spring of 2000. After much discussion, Coach Wiz let me work under assistant Coach Pat to teach me better techniques for speed endurance running. My confidence started to grow under Coach Pat, because I trusted his experience and history.

Coach Pat was an experienced 400m hurdler during his era. He knew that 400m hurdling and 800m running had a close relationship with each other. Competing in outdoor track, 400m hurdlers had the grueling 400m lap plus hurdles and the 800m had the blistering two complete laps of hard running. In fact, you could catch some 400m hurdlers who were just as good at competing in the 800m event, too. Either way, I felt being under the guidance of Coach Pat was where I needed to be.

In the fall of 1999, I just trained and enjoyed my last moments as a senior at Iowa. I participated in activities on and off campus, because I knew my days were numbered as a student-athlete. I took advantage of the free time I had away from cross country competition and continued to attend class. I was scheduled to graduate July 28, 2000, after I completed a mandatory internship program during the summer.

Burn Out!

Everything was in place. It was time to finish out my senior year strong. I thought things were improving in my running career, yet my aggressive edge continued to decline. My joy for running and competing was gradually slipping away. It did not matter how much or how hard I trained. I became less productive.

Coach Wiz constantly asked me "What's wrong?" I had no answer for him. Some of my teammates continued to encourage me while others wrote me off. This was not where I wanted to be in my career. I continued to think back on what it took for me to get to this point.

What was *wrong with me?* I asked myself this question daily. I did not want to give into the thought that I was probably burned out mentally. I tried to move forward with confidence, but the seed of doubt weighed on my mind. I did not even qualify for the finals in the 800m event at the 2000 Indoor Big 10 Championship held at Indiana University, Bloomington.

I also ran a horrible leg on the distance medley relay for our team to score points. It was a disaster. After the Indoor Big 10 Championship, I tried to avoid Coach Wiz. He found me and said, "Even when you are falling short, I still believe in you." He continued to tell me a breakthrough was coming because of the way I trained.

I knew I had it in me, so Coach Wiz and Coach Pat decided to take me to the Indoor NCAA qualifier held at Iowa State. Many runners around the country would use this meet as the last chance to qualify for the Indoor NCAA Track and Field Championship. I knew I had the capability to run at least a 1:48 in the 800m indoors. I just had to bring it out once and for all.

As I headed to Ames, Iowa, I focused on my ability rather than all of my past failures. I wanted to have a clear head in possibly my last indoor race forever. It was time to qualify and erase the past.

There I was in the 800m on Iowa State's 300m indoor track. The race started off well. It was time to prove I was not a failure. I pushed myself hard to finish strong. After I was done, I remember being out of breath. The results were not good. My nightmare continued. I ran a very slow time of 1:57. Embarrassed was not even the word to describe how I felt when I had to face Coach Wiz and Coach Pat.

A 1:57? In my earlier days, I could run a 1:57 in my sleep. Now I was running high school times. No runner expects to go out worse than they come into a program. This was where I was in my collegiate career senior year. A total train wreck! It was like I never had a history of running at all. In my eyes, I was wasted talent. My final indoor track season ended horribly. I had one more track season to go. *What was I going to do?*

The University of Iowa Hosting 1999-2000 Outdoor Big 10 Championships

After the 2000 indoor track season, it was back to the drawing board. The University of Iowa would soon be hosting the 2000 Outdoor Big 10 Track and Field Championship. If I did not qualify for the NCAA Track and Field Championship during the outdoor season, I would finish my season and possibly my running career at the outdoor conference. The championship was scheduled for the weekend of May 19-21, 2000.

The team, the coaching staff, the athletic department, and Iowa City were all looking forward to the experience again. Although my running and competitive nature was in a funk, I was excited as well. I had one more chance to go out with a bang.

The outdoor season kicked off as usual with our spring break trip. We went to Tucson, Arizona. Tucson was very laid back. We got in some good training in Arizona because of the heat. Every year, Iowa City was cold during spring break so we always took advantage of training in either

Arizona or California to start off each season. My training went well, but I still had constant doubts in my mind.

These doubts and fears kept coming up, because even when I trained hard I still competed poorly. I felt like I let my teammates and my school down. I think I spent more time trying to identify where I went wrong over the years. I questioned a lot of things. *Was it my training, diet, or how much rest I gave myself after training? Did it stem from Coach Pat changing my running form? Or maybe it was Coach Wiz telling me how I needed to increase my mileage?* The last possibility I thought about was my ailing foot that was in desperate need of surgery.

It was a frustrating time in my life. This was not why the University of Iowa gave me a chance as a runner. The school wanted results and I was not holding up my end of the agreement. As the season gradually headed toward conference time, there were big meets on our schedule I did not attend during the year in California. Some included the Stanford Invitational, the UCLA Meet, and the Mt. SAC Relays.

You had to be a top performer to compete in meets like these. I was not producing, so I did not go. It was a hard reality to swallow, but I kept moving forward, hoping there would be a breakthrough. The Outdoor Big 10 Championship was still up ahead. Classes were gradually winding down and finals were around the corner.

While I was contemplating my end to running, I also realized that just as quickly as I took my first steps on the university's campus, I was counting down the months before leaving Iowa City. I had no real plans for life after college. I knew I could not go back to Gary, Indiana. How could I go back to where everything started and tell them I was a failure?

The closer I got toward the Big 10 Championship the more I dreaded going to track practices and competing. No matter how hard I trained, my mind was not in it. I was getting worse. I was self-destructing and I did not know where to turn. I couldn't call anyone back home in Gary, because I was too embarrassed to share what I was going through.

I kept a smile on my face, but inside I was frustrated. I started to hear the words "waste of talent" a lot more from some of my teammates. Before, I loved running more than anything. But during this crucial moment in my life, I could not wait for my running career to end. Just a few weeks before the Big 10 Championship, Coach Wiz and I had a one-on-one meeting. I still had no answers for him. It was in this final meeting I decided to walk away from running prior the 2000 Big 10 Championship.

It was one of many hard decisions I had to make. I did not want to embarrass myself or the University of Iowa anymore with the way I competed. Just like that, my collegiate running days were over forever. Time was up.

Running was a vehicle that took me places I never imagined. I was very thankful the University of Iowa gave me the opportunity. Running literally took me across the country. I was able to compete and visit many places such as England, Oregon, Kansas, Arizona, California and Maine. The University of Iowa as a school was phenomenal. I could not have picked a better school to attend. Although I had some failures at the University of Iowa, I was very blessed and fortunate to make a lot of friends and learn more about life. I never took anything for granted. But, it was time to move on with life.

Chapter 14

Life Goes On

Many friends I started college with were graduating. People began moving on with their lives including, getting ready for law school, dental school, and graduate schools across the country. I had no set plans yet while I worked hard my senior year.

As for track, I did not live too far from where the Big 10 Championships were taking place. All of the schools competing were finally in town and the hype of the Big 10 meet was underway. I could not show my face to anyone, so I stayed away from our home track and all the festivities. It was one of the most depressing and disappointing times in my life.

The Internet 1

By the time I was a senior, emails were better than getting handwritten letters in the mail. Every chance I got, I checked my emails at different sites located on campus. I used browsing on the Internet to plan for my next move after college graduation. I knew I could not return home to Gary, so I started making plans to move back to Minnesota.

I wanted to reconnect with my younger siblings Ellis Junior and Faye. The last time I saw them in 1989, they were only babies. I wondered how they were doing each time I competed against the University of Minnesota. The only way I could try to locate them was through their father Ellis Senior. I searched the Internet to locate him. To my surprise, I was able to find a phone number for an Ellis Senior living in Minnesota. I was not sure if I had the correct information, but I left a message on the answering machine anyway.

A few days later I got a call from a man whose voice I didn't recognize too well. He asked me, "Is this Michael, Laura's son?"

"Yes," I replied eagerly. I sat down on my bed.

"This is Ellis Senior, your stepfather," he stated matter-of-factly.

I was stunned for a moment. I could not believe I was talking to him. I stood up and started pacing the short length of my bedroom. Our conversation was very calm. He told me that Ellis Junior and Faye still resided in Minnesota, but they were no longer living with him. He lost all parental rights to them. He even admitted that he abused my little sister Faye, which is what caused him to lose his ability to be part of their lives.

I did not know what to say with this information. After a little more small talk, our conversation ended. I made it my mission to reconnect with Ellis Junior and Faye back in Minnesota. I had no idea how I was going to pull it off, but I knew I would not stop trying until I saw them again.

The Internet 2

I decided to live in Minnesota, but I did not know how I was going to get there and live. I had no real plan in place, no job lined up, or aspirations to continue my education after college. Nevertheless, I could not turn away from my mission. I thought about it until I got an idea.

I remembered my old friend Tone, my teammate who ran AAU track and attended West Side High with me in 1992. Tone and his family moved to Minnesota from Gary, Indiana when I was a freshman in high school. I used the Internet to also locate Tone to see if he still resided in Minnesota. What a blessing, Tone still lived in Minnesota after so many years. I could not believe I reconnected with him. He lived in a single-bedroom apartment. Although he didn't have a lot of room, he instantly welcomed me to come live with him after my college days ended. **(See "A Sad Moment" Chapter 7)**

Graduation Day: July 28th, 2000

Graduation day could not come fast enough. It was a long summer trying to complete my mandatory summer internship. Music helped me through it, especially the album "Heat" by Toni Braxton. I listened to this album when I needed to take my mind off the frustrations I was dealing with.

As the big day crept up, I learned that my family from Gary, Indiana and Chicago, Illinois would not be attending my graduation ceremony. I knew part of it was my fault. I caused a lot of pain when I ran away from home at the age of fifteen. Marie still held onto some of the frustration. She felt that I honored people that were in my life temporarily. In doing that, she felt dishonored even though she made the ultimate sacrifice of taking me and my siblings in back in 1989.

Marie periodically let me know that she had been there for me since the day I was born. She was justifiably angry. But I could not forget all the people who helped me along the way. In one of our Iowa Hawkeye press guides the team released every year, Miss Price was listed as my mother. Marie took this as a slap in the face when she read it. My godmother felt that she or at least my biological mother Laura should have been listed in the booklet. I did not try to offend anyone and it was an honest mistake, but it was one I couldn't fix.

I walked across the stage on July 28, 2000 with my chin up. Even if my family wasn't there to cheer me on, I was proud of myself. As I was handed the diploma I smiled. This was a good day.

After the ceremony was over, a little sadness crept in. It was depressing having no one at my graduation ceremony. I thought about my mother Laura. I knew she would have been proud but I had no clue if she was alive or dead. I believed I would see her again so I could tell her she had a son who graduated from college. It was a major stepping stone in our family.

I did get a graduation gift from a good friend of mine named Kelly Drools. She'd always supported me during my years at Iowa. Kelly remembered birthdays and other special occasions. She and her mom gave me some money, which helped me move to Minnesota. I was also able to budget some of the student loan I borrowed for the summer. I planned my own celebration at the home I resided in my senior year. I partied with some of my classmates on campus who were either there for the summer or who graduated with me.

My lease ended in July, so I had a short time to get my belongings together to move. I was officially finished with school, and it was almost time to leave Iowa City. As I packed up everything I owned into medium sized brown cardboard boxes, I stopped to look at a couple of photos pinned to the wall above my bed. They were of me at some of the places I was able to compete at and visit around America. One included Oregon where I was able to run past the accident site of legendary runner Steve Prefontaine.

I continued to look at more pictures. I had a photo of legendary writer Stephen King's home. I had a lot to be proud of because not too many people could say they saw Stephen King's home in Maine. All of the photos were memories I would keep as long as I could.

Me after graduation

Me waiting to be called

Getting Packed

Some of my teammates still remained in Iowa for the summer. They let me stay with them after my lease was up. I looked forward to a new start. I planned to meet Tone in Minnesota on the day of my departure. Everything was in motion.

When that day arrived, I rented a one-way U-Haul truck with no insurance on it. I had little money for gas, a credit card with a five hundred dollar limit, and an Indiana State driver's license. It didn't matter. I was excited knowing that I would soon see my siblings again. When I closed the door to the U-Haul truck, I soaked in Iowa City for the last time.

Although I still had some regrets, I was very thankful for my college experience. I enjoyed so many moments during my time in Iowa, but it was time to go.

CHAPTER 15

BACK TO MINNESOTA

In August of 2000, I headed back to Minnesota. The trip took five hours. The entire time I drove I thought about how excited I was to get back to Minnesota for good. I did not have a cell phone, so I had to keep pulling over on the highway to use a pay phone. Tone and I planned to meet at a central location when I arrived.

I sat inside the U-Haul waiting for Tone once I'd made it to our meeting point. He pulled up in a 1997 purple Toyota Corolla wearing shades. I grinned and nodded my head down to indicate I saw him. He pulled his car in front of me and waved for me to follow him. We drove a few miles to the nearest storage facility in Brooklyn Park. He'd chosen it because it was not too far from his apartment complex.

When Tone and I finally had a chance to catch up, I noticed he had gained weight. He was no longer the cross country runner I remembered him as. He was more cut with a little more muscle. He reached for a box I'd just unloaded from the back of the U-Haul. "Thanks, man," I said then wiped the sweat from my forehead.

"I only have enough money to keep my things in storage for two months, so I have to start looking for a job," I said carrying the box into storage. As we continued unpacking, I told Tone about how soon I was going to have to pay back the student loan I borrowed to finish school as well. Tone closed the pull down door to the rental unit and locked it. "Don't worry. I'll hook you up at my job. You can work with me there."

I had to start from scratch. I could not believe what I went from. I was recently a student-athlete at one of the biggest schools in the country. Now I slept on Tone's couch in his single-bedroom apartment. It was embarrassing. I could not blame anyone but myself.

The Real World (Part 1)

All of a sudden, there were no more track practices, no more classes, no more campus activities and no more college. I was in the real world. Nothing was going to come free or easy as it did for me in college. I had a five thousand dollar student loan to pay back and things in storage I had to pay for monthly. I still had no idea how I was going to make contact with my siblings either. I had no car or my own place to live. There was work to do.

Tone and Me in later years

Tone took me under his wing. He was placed in my life at the right time. We already had a foundation in our friendship, because of cross country and track and field. That helped us live together easier. I put in an application where he worked. It was not the kind of job I was looking for after college, but it was better than nothing. Responsibilities were adding up, and I had no other opportunities. My job interview was horrible. If it were not for Tone speaking up on my behalf, I would not have been hired otherwise. He already knew my work ethic. Tone knew I would not let him down once I got the job.

Once I got in, I took advantage of earning wages, especially after being a broke college student. I worked hard. In a relatively short time, I made enough money to pay back my student loan, give Tone half the rent money for his apartment, and buy a new 2000 Nissan Sentra.

The possibilities seemed limitless as long as I put in the work and stayed focused. I was twenty three years old and having too much fun. I made a good living. Every other night I went to a different club in Minneapolis or St. Paul. I constantly chased the women in Minnesota. Now that I had my own transportation and cell phone, there was no stopping me. I remained responsible in many ways, but lived careless in others. Thanking God was nowhere on my radar. I was having a good time and hadn't thought about the Bible verses I learned from Coach Tiny in years.

The Real World (Part 2)

When I was in a better position, I started reaching out to Ellis Junior and Faye. Making contact with Ellis Junior was relatively easy. He lived in foster care not too far from my residence. Each time before I could visit him, I had to get special permission from his social worker. I kept the lines of communication open with his social worker so I could see my little brother often.

On the other hand, spending time with my little sister Faye was a very sensitive and difficult process. She was in her teenage years, and handled many traumatic issues growing up. Faye resided in a home specialized for girls who dealt with abusive issues. Faye had a lot of anger and emotional problems I was not aware of. Her social worker would not allow me to come into her life as easily as I did with Ellis Junior.

The government worker did not want Faye to have to recuperate from someone who might leave her life shortly after reentering it. That was never my intent, but I understood why her protector was cautious of me. Overall, the process of seeing my youngest siblings was a new experience. I had to be patient and gradually work my way back into their lives.

I was not able to be a legal guardian over them, but I wanted to at least reach out to them and let them know I was there. I didn't get permission to see Faye in person, but we talked on the phone. During our conversations Faye had so many questions for me. Some of her questions were difficult to answer right away. I could tell she was hurt and confused.

In one of our conversations Faye told me she cried many nights wondering about our mom. She did not have any memories of her. I heard the pain in her voice. At the time, I wished I could give her a hug. There was nothing I could do but listen to her and share words of comfort and encouragement.

Through it all, Faye still believed she would meet our mother one day. I continued to tell her things would be okay. Well I hoped so, knowing I had no status of my mom. I had no real answers for Ellis Junior and Faye, but I was going to do my best to bridge that gap between our family.

The Real World (Part 3)

In addition to growing in my relationship with my two siblings, I continued to succeed at work. Tone and I both assisted each other financially. We decided to become roommates and moved into a two-bedroom apartment in Richfield, Minnesota.

The apartment was not the best but it was better than living in a one-bedroom. I finally had my own room and did not have to sleep on Tone's couch anymore. Our commute to work was even closer. We thought we had it made. Tone's parents were like my parents, too. The Spears Family took me in as their son. Tone's mom was always there when we needed her, but most of the time Tone and I handled things on our own.

I also started picking up Ellis Junior some weekends so we could spend time together. I was still unable to see my sister Faye in person but we continued to keep in touch by phone. Everything was a process when it came to Faye. All I could do was remain patient.

In 2002 I was finally able to see Faye in person. She lived in foster care on the south side of Minneapolis. Ellis Junior had too many problems in his home. He was placed in another house for boys in Anoka, Minnesota.

Seeing Ellis Junior became a challenge when he relocated. It took me more than an hour to visit him in Anoka so I could not see him as much as before. A long time passed before I could see both Ellis Junior and Faye together at the same time.

When I finally did, it was like a wish come true. I instantly recognized they both shared a special bond with each other. Ellis Junior and Faye were all they knew growing up. They had a closeness that was unbreakable. Even with their bond, I could feel a lot of frustration inside of them, too. I knew I had some more work to do, but at least we were getting somewhere.

The Real World (Part 4-Mid 2002)

Besides dealing with improving Ellis Junior and Faye's relationship, my manager Mr. Jeff wanted me to move up in the company. He told me I had a great deal of potential. He did not want to hold me back from opportunities within the company. I was resistant at first and unsure if I was up to the challenge. Ultimately, I climbed the corporate ladder and worked on a very good team within the company. I earned more money than I ever expected. I had a serious girlfriend. Life was getting better . . . until I got the call.

CHAPTER 16

GOING TO PANAMA JUNE 2002

One day my cousin Candy called and told me that my family in Panama finally caught up with my mother Laura. Candy went on to say that my mother was in a hospital dying from AIDS. It felt like my heart stopped the moment I heard the news. I thought I was dreaming at first but everything was real. I wondered, *AIDS? Is she going to die before I get a chance to see her again? How am I going to share this with Ellis Junior and Faye?*

My mind was full of questions. I knew I had to get to Panama, but I did not know how to do it in such short notice. Besides, I'd never been to Panama. I cried the entire night after getting the bad news. My mother was in pain and there was nothing I could do. It seemed like she suffered her whole life.

When I shared the news with my new manager Mr. Smith, he was very supportive. He allowed me to use some of my company time to figure out how to visit my mother. I renewed my passport. My girlfriend at the time was more supportive. She gave me the extra six hundred dollars I needed to book the last minute plane ticket.

God watched over me and made provisions even if I didn't realize He was doing it. Everything worked out smoothly when it was time to leave the country. I flew out of Newark, New Jersey, which was not too far from where the terrorist attacks of 9/11 took place. The incident was still fresh around the world, so flying over New York and New Jersey was a very chilling experience.

When I looked outside the plane, I knew a lot of lives were lost right below. It was a day I will never forget. As I thought of that horrible time, I also thought of my mother and how desperate I was to see her.

Reuniting with Laura (Part 1)

I made it to Panama after six hours of flying. I was in the country where both my mother and father were born. It was hard to believe that I too was almost born in Panama back in 1977. Soon after walking on Panamanian soil, I wanted to go back to America. This land was different, and I was out of my comfort zone. The air was not only hot and humid. It was also polluted. There was no turning back though. I had to remember the mission I was on. I was headed to see my mother, for possibly the last time.

Some of my family members who lived in Colón, Panama waited for me at the airport's exit gate. There were so many people standing around waiting for family and friends. The scene was like one I'd watched in dozens of movies. Clusters of people stood around chatting. When whomever they were waiting for got off the plane that group erupted in cheers like they'd just seen a famous star.

Out of the crowd my mother's sister, Aunt Estelle, called to me when I approached the exit. So many years had passed since I'd last seen her in the United States. She still had that same gold tooth in her mouth I remembered very well. When I finally was close enough, she gave me the biggest hug. I was in good hands with my family in

Panama. We had another two hours of traveling before getting to Colón. I counted down the hours before seeing my mother Laura again.

When I arrived in Colón, I stayed with my Uncle Nesto, his wife Dora, and my cousins in their home. Uncle Nesto was the first of many uncles who welcomed me. He looked exactly like my Grandfather Wynston. We had so much to talk about. Everyone sat around his home and caught up on a lot of stories since I had to wait one more day to see my mom. I did not realize how many relatives I had in Panama. It was almost overwhelming to see another side of my family. I had cousins who could speak English and Spanish fluently. It was amazing!

The next day my cousins took me to the center where my mother resided. The outside of the facility was very clean and secure. Since I was around twelve years old when I last hugged her, I was extremely anxious to see my mom after so many years. When my cousins and I entered through the gated door, it was cool and kept up well on the inside, too.

"Wait here," the worker who let us in told my family. She pointed her hand towards a waiting room. We sat down in the room while she went to get my mother prepared. I was just moments away from seeing Laura again. My heart continued to beat faster and faster in anticipation.

My cousin Alfred asked me, "Are you scared?"

I said "No." I was ready to see my mother again. The center worker finally came into the waiting room where we all passed the time.

"Michael," she said slowly. A smile lit up her face. "Laura is ready to see you." I went to the appropriate door. Before I could open it all the way, I saw a very sick man in another room lying in bed. There were several nurses who stood right in front of me as I slowly walked through the entry. They all had matching grins on their faces. Before I went any further, I turned my head slightly to the left. My mother was standing directly behind the door. I immediately noticed she looked nothing like I recalled. She was short and very slim, standing there in her hospital robe. When she said her first words to me, I noticed a deep Spanish accent I did not recognize at all.

One thing I did remember was that smile she always had. It never changed. It was warm and welcoming. She instantly touched my face when I returned her joyful expression. She said, "Michael, my son!" I then gave her the biggest hug. While I was holding her, I could feel her rib cages through the hospital robe. It was like embracing a skeleton. My mother was indeed sick but for that moment I did not care. I was holding her again.

We had much to catch up on. There were so many questions I wanted to ask. I did not know if this would be the last time we would speak again. When we went back to the waiting room, my mother and I sat very close to each other. She held onto my hands. Every once in a while she rubbed my chest like I was a little baby.

My cousins and my half-brother Pepito were all in the same room with us. They listened to me as I talked to my mom. I was so caught in the moment I could not even tell you what I said to her.

My cousin Alfred asked my mother, "Laura, are you now going to stop your fast lifestyle?" When he questioned my mother, I knew exactly what he meant. *Would she discontinue making bad choices with her life?*

My mother started to cry as she nodded her head yes. There was not a dry eye in the waiting room. You could feel all the emotions after my cousin's question. He, too, was tired of seeing my mother suffer. A lot of her pain came

Michael Layne

from the poor choices she made in life. Alfred helped my mother realize that even with all of her mistakes, she still had a son who loved her.

That was a fact. I never gave up on my mother. I knew she made some bad decisions in her life, but I in no way stopped loving her, even in her long absence. I could not turn my back on her, in spite of the fact that she'd turned her back on us. As a child I was too young to fully understand why she had to go. I just remembered being with my mother through her many struggles in the U.S. I knew what she went through and what she had to endure. It was time to have that intimate mother and son conversation once and for all.

"Mom," I said in a little boy voice. "Why were you deported back to Panama?"

She looked down at her hands then replied, "Everything had to do with drugs. I was given two choices after I was caught selling and using drugs by the authorities." She paused for a moment then continued. "I could spend fifteen years in prison in the U.S. or go back to Panama where I would remain until fifteen years were up. I would rather live in my home country than live in prison with no freedom for fifteen years."

I took her hands in mine. She continued to tell me that it was a hard decision to make in her late twenties. She felt her six children would be in good hands with family in the United States. My mother had no idea the damage that would take place in our lives based on her quick decision. Her choice affected each one of her kids, including me. As the saying goes, we have choices but we cannot choose the consequences after we make a choice.

I knew my mother was feeling the pain deep in her heart because of what she had done. I really could not imagine how much suffering she was dealing with. It would be hard for a mother to leave her kids behind, but I understood why it was easy for her to turn to drugs. They took her mind off of the pain for the moment, but the pain never went away. She needed that constant high to get through life.

Mom and Me reunited after many years

My half-brother Pepito and Me

Reuniting with Laura (Part 2)

I was never mad at my mom. I was very excited to see her, and I wanted to make things right. As we continued our mother and son conversation, I told her many things about my life. I spoke about all of her children, my high school days, my college days, and my dating experiences. I even mentioned my favorite musical artist Faith Evans and my track and field days.

Since I did not know how much longer she was going to live, I wanted her to have as much information as possible. The amount of time she had left on earth was up to God. However, I wanted her to live as long as possible. I started to plan in my head how I could help her while I lived in Minnesota. I knew AIDS was nothing to take lightly, and she needed medication to extend her life. I asked a lot of questions to see what I could do. I could not leave Panama without some type of action plan in place to help my mom.

After spending time with my mother, I left the center and headed for another family reunion. I was going to finally meet my father's side of the family, too. My father, Pedro Avila, died in May of 1999. I was a few years short of meeting him in person. My paternal grandmother was eagerly expecting my arrival though. Her name was Paula and she didn't work too far from the center where my mother currently resided.

When I met my Grandmother Paula, she said something in Spanish to me. Then she placed her fingers over my eyebrows. My cousin told me my grandmother said I had the same eyebrow features as my father, Pedro. All of my cousins on my father's side had thick eyebrows. It was confirmed. I was an Avila. Paula kept telling me in a teasing way, "Your name should be Miguel Avila." I could do nothing but smile.

She started introducing me to many of my other cousins that passed by her job. Before I knew it, I was meeting a lot of my family right there in Colón. I never knew I had so many aunts and uncles. The only hard part for me was that they barely spoke English. They asked me questions in Spanish. I could not understand them. My Spanish teachers from West Side High would have been very disappointed in me. It was almost as if I did not learn anything in school. I could not say a word back to my family in Spanish. Before I left my Grandmother Paula for the day, she told my cousin a message to tell me. In English my cousin explained, "Your grandmother wants to spend a whole day with you before you leave Panama."

Paula wanted to cook for me and tell me things about my father. I only had a few more days before it was time to go back to America. I made sure to plan the rest of my trip in a way where I could still spend as much time as possible with all of my family. It was exciting to see the history I had in Panama.

I also did some sightseeing. My Uncle Nesto took me to visit the Panama Canal where he and many of my family members were employed. It was where my great grandfather David and grandfather Wynston used to work.

Hanging out in Panama with family

My paternal grandmother Paula

My uncle took me to the Panama Canal to take pictures

Panama Canal loading a ship

Hanging out with my family drinking
Coconut Water in Panama

Going Back to the U.S.

I must've had about a hundred mosquito bites all over my body. I got eaten alive after 5 p.m. each day. My family teased me a lot about my marks, because I was paranoid about getting bitten. They said mosquitoes knew when sweet blood was around. I kept a bottle of calamine lotion and witch hazel with me at all times. I wanted to avoid scratching them and risking an infection.

As my time in Panama was coming to an end, I said my final goodbyes to my family. The hardest thing for me to do was to go see my mother for possibly the last time. She could not leave the center to go with me to the airport because of her weak condition. I had to say goodbye to her at the facility. We shared another mother and son conversation. She started to cry. Her eyes were so brown and full of sadness. I held back my own tears, and told her, "This is not a goodbye. I will come back to see you again."

My mother finally cheered up and stopped her gentle sobbing. I had a good plan in place that would help her while I was away. I promised to send her money for medication twice a month so she could gradually get back on her feet. It would be a slow process but I needed my mother to believe she could do it.

As I was leaving the center, my mother encouraged me to try to come back for Panama's Independence Day festivities in November. I knew I could not make it back the same year, but I would definitely give it a shot to return the following year. For now, it was time to go back home to Minnesota and soak in my first experience in Panama.

CHAPTER 17

BACK HOME IN MINNESOTA

I couldn't wait to share my Panama experience with my friends and co-workers when I arrived back in Minnesota. I explained how my family had a rich history of working for the Panama Canal. I was more appreciative and thankful for my life after leaving my mom's country. I could not believe I'd visited one of the poorest countries in the world. My family made it through such harsh conditions.

I was grateful for all the sacrifices that were made just for me to become a U.S. citizen. One of my long term visions at the time was to take a few high school students from the United States to visit Panama. I wanted kids to see the struggles of Panamanian life. Hearing someone's story is one thing, but experiencing it first hand is life changing.

Moving Up, Moving Forward

I stuck to my plan and started sending my mother money. I had to keep things on a tight budget financially, because Western Union was very expensive. I consistently did well at work. Opportunities seemed as if they were always available. My manager Mr. Smith decided I was ready for a different challenge. He encouraged me to take a higher position within the company, too. This meant more money and more experience in the corporate world.

By this time, Tone and I worked in different departments. We were still close. I owed Tone a lot, and I was thankful to him for how he helped me over the years. We remained roommates until he got married. Then it was time to go our separate ways.

I moved into a one-bedroom apartment. I became a true bachelor, but still took care of my mom. I had peace of mind knowing that she was getting stronger and recovering. Things were going very well in my life. I was humble because I knew everything it took for me to get to this point.

I started to venture out and try new things in Minneapolis. I remained at my job but also worked at a neighboring Foot Locker to get discounts on clothes and shoes. Additionally, I volunteered at a local radio station from 10 p.m. to 2 a.m. I had always been a fan of slow R&B music. My days consisted of working at my full-time job, then selling shoes at Foot Locker, followed by volunteering at a local radio station.

I loved disk jockeying the music at night with a radio personality named Lady L. Before I could work there alone, I had to prove to Lady L that I was skilled at playing old school and new school R&B music. She quickly trained me on how to use the board to control the music. Once Lady L saw that I had an ear for music, she gave me my radio personality name *Magic,* because I was magical at setting the mood for the late night listeners.

I could not believe I was on live radio entertaining people with my style of play. It was cool to get calls from listeners. They let me know I was making their day or doing a good job. I made a little name for myself and enjoyed a small amount of fame. As always, I was very thankful just to get the opportunity to be on the radio.

What Goes Up . . .

Things were consistently looking up. I got another promotion at work. Financially I was doing way more than I ever expected. Between the years 2003 and 2004, I was able to purchase a single-family town home in one of the many suburbs of Minneapolis. It was a major step in my life under the age of thirty. I was blessed and very fortunate.

Thinking back to August 2000, I could not believe I went from sleeping on Tone's couch to now owning my own home. On top of everything else, I was still taking care of my mother. She was now living comfortably with her medical condition. I was able to visit her in Panama four more times. I was finally able to attend Panama's Independence Festivities in November of 2003. I visited twice in 2005. The first visit was in February for Panama's Carnival Festivities. In November I went to Panama's Independence Festivities.

Each time I visited my mom, she looked better than the trip before. Her hair grew longer, she gained weight, and she was going to church to keep her mind off the streets. I was very proud of my mom and her recovery. I did not have that true, one-on-one relationship with God just yet, but I was still grateful to Him because He spared her life. She was on her death bed in 2002. Now she was very active and living a normal life.

She even started dating someone with her same condition. My mom was a sucker for love, but she was happy. She and her new boyfriend Samuel even shared a place together in Panama. The fourth time I went to Panama was to visit them in their new home. I was happy my mother finally had a place of her own.

She was able to cook every meal for me in the comfort of her home. We haven't shared moments like that since the 1980's. Back then she always cooked hot oatmeal or Cream of Wheat for those harsh winters we had in the Midwest. It was so good to see my mother throwing down in the kitchen. She still had it!

It was obvious that she enjoyed just being a mom again. She missed out on many years of all of her children's lives, so it felt great for her just to take care of me. As a son, I sat back and pretended to be that little kid again while my mother did her motherly duties. It made her feel good. I wish my siblings were there to enjoy the same things I did but finances were tight for everyone. I hoped that one day all of my siblings and I would reunite as a family and visit her.

Mom and Me years later after her recovery

Must Come Down

From 2000-2005, everything was solid. I finally felt stable for once in my life. I was growing in just about every area except spiritually. I knew God was tugging at my heart, but I did not want to change my lifestyle. I kept lying to God and myself saying I would change my ways before submitting to Him. The word "saved" kept coming back to me, but I still had no clue what the word meant.

Even the little bit that I did wasn't enough for me to change my ways. I went to church when I felt like it. Although God continued to provide for me, I gave Him no real credit. I thought I was making things happen because of my own will. Then things in my life started to fall apart slowly.

My relationship with Ellis Junior and Faye became very distant. They were growing up. I felt they held onto anger with me for how they grew up. They were part of the main reasons I relocated back to Minnesota. I wanted to be close to them, and gradually reunite everyone. But my plan did not go so well.

I may have been closer to them than my other siblings physically, but mentally and emotionally I got some of their frustrations. They really suffered from a lot of things growing up. They had deep inner pains I did not know how to handle. I simply could not reach them. Too much damage had been done to them in their younger years.

Another person in my life that started doing worse was my mother. She started hanging back in the streets in Panama. Some of my family members there called me. They let me know that they saw her from time to time hanging around people known for doing drugs. I knew it was easy for her to relapse into that lifestyle, but I did not want to believe it. We had come so far since my first visit to Panama.

When I contacted her by phone, she always told me everything was okay. I finally got the message that she indeed fell back into the drug lifestyle. This happened when I could no longer contact her as quickly as I could before by phone. I had no real proof, but I knew something was wrong. It was a gut feeling I had. I wanted my suspicions to be wrong, because my mother had come from a near death experience in 2002. I hoped that she remembered this and turned away from whatever had her attention.

Not only was my youngest siblings and mother's life not going well, one of my favorite activities had to stop. I ended my time volunteering at the local radio station due to a management change. One of the managers wanted me to play only suggested music from a playlist and nothing more. The creativity and the fun were taken away. I decided not to volunteer four hours of my time to play a music list someone gave me. The experience was great, but time was up.

I also spent some of my time outside of work in relationships with women for the wrong reasons. I was constantly doing what I wanted to do, no questions asked. I dated for a moment. When the relationship ended I was on to the next woman. I thought, *I'm on top of the world.*

This area of my life was inconsistent. I had some deep and major insecurities I could not shake. Many times my relationships were unhealthy. I upset some women, and I got my feelings injured. Before a woman could hurt me, I would cause the pain. If I got wronged, the next woman would pay. I completely failed in this area of my life.

Just when I thought my life could not get any worse, my company decided to close their doors in Minnesota. This was when I started to learn about the business world.

Things can change at any given moment to meet industry demands. I was only in my new home for little over a year. There were several questions I had each day and no real answers. *What was I going to do with my home? What choices did I have? Did I have to start over? Was this the end of the road?* Things were falling apart in my life from all angles. I had no clue what I was going to do next.

Divine Detour Unseen

All of my co-workers had decisions to make. We had the option to relocate to another state where the company had a site. I could also take advantage of school opportunities in Minnesota, look for another job, or get a severance package. Decisions had to be made by New Year's Eve, 2006.

Time was ticking for everyone. The idea of relocating to another state was not in my original plan. I had grown comfortable in Minnesota. I knew where things were, and I felt stable in my new home. Relocating was out of the question. I decided to stick it out and remain in Minnesota.

But, when reality hit, my decision to stay in my current zip code changed. Many of my peers chose to relocate to another state. The company was big in South Carolina, Colorado, Arizona and Texas. The idea of relocating didn't look so bad. Part of my life was spent relocating anyway so it was really nothing new to me. I quickly narrowed my choices down to where I could see myself residing.

I chose Colorado and Texas. I got a small taste of South Carolina back in my college visiting days. When I attended the University of Iowa, I was able to visit Arizona on more than one occasion. Neither state was appealing to me.

Colorado was beautiful when I had the opportunity to visit, but something was pointing me in the direction of Texas.

I was fortunate to take a quick visit to Dallas, Texas before I had to make a final decision. That visit sealed the deal. Texas was going to be my new home. Although I didn't enjoy the heat there, I could really see new things for my life in the Lone Star State. All I had to do was map out a plan of how I could keep things in order in Minnesota before I moved. I had to carefully make a choice between putting my new home on the market for sale or renting it out. I did not know how this Texas thing would play out, so I looked at the option of renting my home just in case I needed to return to Minnesota.

I give much thanks to my supervisor Sylvia and Human Resources for really setting me up for a smooth transition to Texas. It helped that I had good history with the company. Everything was set up perfectly. All I had to do was get there and continue working hard. A good friend and co-worker named Norman also decided to relocate to the same company branch. We decided to become roommates. Before I knew it, I was Texas-bound!

Chapter 18

Plan Predicted

I said my last goodbyes to family and friends before I did my final packing. I promised to keep in contact with Ellis Junior and Faye while I lived in Texas. They both understood and supported my decision. I had a realtor in place to help me manage my property after I moved away. All we had to do was find renters. When all of my packing was done, my home was very clean and empty. I laid my garage door opener on the bottom steps of my home. I couldn't believe I was moving on with my life yet again.

Although I was very excited about moving to Texas, the doubts entered my mind. I was unsure how things would go. My high school teammate Ed, who became a pastor in Gary, told me God had so much in store for me in Texas.

It was no shock that he would be preaching the word of God. Coach Tiny saw the potential in him to become a pastor when we were in high school. I used to always say, "Ed will have a boring job if he becomes a pastor." Church was dull to me, so I thought if Ed became a pastor, he would be uninteresting, too. Yet again, I was totally thinking opposite from God's plan.

As an adult, I valued Ed's opinion. He prophesied I would meet my wife in my new home state. He also said she would be celibate, and my lifestyle of bad habits would change because of this woman. I believed my longtime friend about meeting a woman. However, getting married without having sex first made no sense to me. I kept telling myself sex was a must. Marriage was not on my agenda. I did not see myself being committed, let alone being married. I felt something was wrong with Ed, but he was like a big brother to me, and I trusted him.

On the Road Again:
The Exodus from Minnesota

It was a cool early morning on November 29, 2006. I got in a U-Haul truck to travel one-way. I held onto enough things to furnish an apartment. My car sat on top of an auto-transport that was attached to the back of the rental. As I drove off, I took one final look at my house. In a matter of moments, it was out of sight.

I headed toward highway 35W going south. It was going to be a long fifteen to sixteen hour drive to Texas. The climate conditions remained chilly, but the sun was out, and the roads were clear. I had an atlas in the passenger seat, and I was on the road again.

A sluggish four hours went by. I thought I was making good time until I realized I was still driving through Iowa. The cold temperatures were still steady as I headed toward Nebraska. Each time I passed through a city, I marked where I was on the atlas. I made sure I was on the right path to get to my destination.

When I traveled out of Nebraska, the skies started to get dark. I made it to Kansas City, Kansas during their rush hour. The weather continued to get worse. I did not want to get into an accident with the U-Haul truck and my car attached to the back. It was nerve-wrecking. I made sure everything was still in place as I drove with my car attached to the auto-transport. I was extra careful not to make any sharp turns and to remember there was something linked to the rental. It was then that I developed great respect for the truck driving profession and what truck drivers had to go through on a daily basis.

The mission to get to Texas continued. As I was leaving Kansas City, it looked like a storm was brewing in the sky. I pulled over at a gas station to fill up. The clerk told me Kansas was expecting a major snow storm. This was no big thing to me coming from Minnesota. My former home state always had snow storms. The clerk got my attention when she said, "Kansas does not have the clean-up crew like Minnesota does."

In other words, I could be driving on roads that were slippery. There would be no salt placed on the ground for traction like I was used to. I thought, *Uh Oh!* I immediately pumped seventy dollars worth of gas so I could get out of Kansas. I was determined to make it to Oklahoma and beat the snow storm. I thought the closer I headed south the better off I would be from the storm. I was wrong. The weather got worse as I continued to drive south. The skies grew darker, and the roads were getting slick.

I kept moving. I figured I would get a break in the weather, but it did not let up. The sight of cars in ditches with their hazard lights on increased. I realized it was time to get off the road. According to my atlas, I was halfway to Dallas, Texas anyway. I had another eight hours to go. I did not want to risk it. I finally gave in and pulled over to the nearest hotel I could find.

When I got out of the U-Haul, the grounds along with my car were covered in ice. It was freezing in Kansas! I finally checked in at the local hotel. The lady at the front desk told me Kansas had not seen this type of weather in over twenty five years. I thought, *Out of all the time in the world, why did this weather have to hit now? Was I bringing the cold weather with me from Minnesota?* I don't know. All I did know was that I could not go anywhere for the remainder of the night.

Snowing in Texas

On November 30, 2006, I woke up extra early in my hotel room. I looked through the windows at the weather conditions outside. Everything seemed normal for driving. I got my things together, checked out of the hotel, and got back on the road before early morning traffic picked up. I continued to believe if I drove farther south, the flurry conditions would disappear. I was wrong again!

By the time I made it to Oklahoma, the weather was atrocious. Snow covered everything. It was hard to see through the glass. I had to roll down the side windows of the U-Haul just to get a quick visual of what was ahead. The storm seemed like it was following me. I had no other choice but to drive thirty to fifty miles per hour.

It was a long slow drive, but I kept moving through the storm. My trip was seriously delayed. I had to make it to Dallas by 5 p.m. to sign my apartment lease. That's when the main office of the apartment complex closed for the day. If I did not make it in time, I would have to get another hotel room for the night. Funds were running low. The U-Haul was eating at least seventy dollars each gas stop. Plus, I had to make sure I had enough money to fill up the truck before I turned it back in.

When I finally crossed over into the north part of my new home state, I was shocked. It was snowing in Texas!

I pulled over to fill up again. Next I texted some of my friends back in Minnesota to tell them about this sight. I expected to see sunshine and feel heat like I did on my first visit. As I continued to drive, I saw several car accidents along the route. It was almost as if the car crashes were at every bridge.

I did not think driving on ice was a big deal coming from Minnesota. But, many people in Texas did not know how to drive on frost covered slippery roads. I finally made it to Dallas safe and sound. It was the grace of God that protected me through the wintery conditions to get to my destination . . . but I did not realize this right away.

The New Start

I made it to Trinity Apartments just in time to sign my new lease and get the keys. I thought driving almost a full day was tiresome. When I found out where I would be living, I had a more exhausting task ahead of me. My new home was on the third floor, located in the back of the complex. There were no elevators either. First I removed the auto-transport attachment from the U-Haul. Next I had to carry all of my belongings up three flights of stairs then straight to the back. I kept going up and down the stairs, getting the workout of a lifetime. It was very cold. It was North Texas's first ice storm of 2006. I was moving right in the heart of it!

I saved my bed mattress as the last piece of furniture to carry up the stairs. A lady was going home to her apartment. She saw me carrying this huge mattress up the narrow stairs. She stopped what she was doing and helped me. We got the mattress to the top of the third floor. I told the lady thank you. I was worn out mentally and physically from driving and lifting things. After my mission was complete, I drove to a local Wal-Mart. I bought new sheets, new pillows, and the movie *Superman Returns.* I hooked up my television and DVD player. Then I made the bed, took the hottest shower, and finally turned on the movie. When I laid down, I fell fast asleep.

Chapter 19

The Brewing of God's Plan

I was scheduled to work on Monday, December 4, 2006. To avoid getting lost or being late for work, I decided to make an early visit to the company that weekend. I wanted to see where it was located and how long it would take for me to commute there. On the Saturday before I started work, I got in my gray Nissan Maxima and drove from Irving to North Dallas. The drive took me about twenty to twenty five minutes to arrive there. I quickly familiarized myself with all the routes and highways to get to and from work.

On my first day, I met a lot of my new co-workers and managers. Things were a little different as I expected them to be. I started to miss the days in Minnesota, but there was no turning back. I made it my mission to continue the same success I had in my former home state. One thing that brought me comfort was seeing so many beautiful ladies. My eyes were all over the place. I began to realize that adjusting to Dallas life might not be so bad after all.

I got a call from my cousin Alfonzo who lived in Chicago this same weekend. He stated he and his wife Nissa were coming to Texas. They both called to let me know they were on their way to Dallas for business. They wanted to see me. I was new in the DFW Metroplex so it felt comforting to know I would be around family soon.

I told Nissa to call me when they arrived in town. Some of my co-workers gave me the inside scoop of where to go and what things to do in Texas. I wanted to get to the nearest gym just to start toning up. My peers told me about a place that only cost five dollars to get in as long as I lived in Irving. It was a small recreation center, but it would have to do until I found a bigger gym. I made plans to attend that facility on December 5, 2006, immediately upon finishing my day at work.

Alfonzo and Nissa called me once they arrived in town. It was right after I got off work. They invited me to go to dinner with them. Nissa was very familiar with the area since she once lived in Texas. She had a good friend who was also joining them for dinner. I really did not want to go. I told them I needed to catch up with them another day.

Nissa encouraged me to meet this friend of hers. Exercising was my main priority though. We ended our conversation after I mentioned I would call her after I finished exercising. When I arrived at the gym, it was closed for the day. I called Nissa back and said I would join them for dinner after all. They offered to pick me up from my apartment complex. We also had to get Nissa's good friend from her home before we went to dinner. Our plans for the evening were set.

The Introduction of God's Plan

So there we were. Alfonzo, Nissa and I traveling somewhere (I thought was too far) to pick up this special friend of hers. We were on highway 360 going south during rush hour. The skies were getting dark. I took small naps, because traffic was backed up for miles. I kept telling myself, *I wish I would have stayed home and hung out with my family another*

179

time. I was still drained from "car lag" after driving from Minnesota to Texas just a few days prior. A nice nap in my own bed after work sounded real nice.

As usual, there was no turning back to my apartment complex. I was stuck like chuck. We finally arrived at our destination. It was still early in the day, but the skies were dark. It seemed like we were in the car for hours. Nissa was very excited that she was going to see this good friend of hers. She bragged about her friend constantly. I thought, *This friend better be worth the trip, because it took us forever to get to her house.*

I deserved to see what the friend looked like. I wore a tie that day so I fixed it before we walked to mystery lady's door. When it opened up, I heard the biggest southern accent I will never forget. "Hello!" Nissa quickly entered this woman's home and gave her friend the biggest hug. I was the last person to enter.

When I finally made eye contact with this woman, she said "Hello, my name is Ericka." I told her my name. My immediate thought was that she was beautiful, but she was "one of those!" I thought she was a bougie girl. That is someone who knows she is beautiful but would not give you the time of day. Erika had this confident attitude about herself.

Nissa made comments about the home as Erika gave us a quick tour. Then the women went to her bedroom. Ericka talked about how she painted her own walls. When I heard what she said, I immediately looked at my cousin with a smirk. I remarked, "Yeah Right!" The designs were beautiful and looked like they were professionally done. I did not believe this bougie girl did her own painting so I continued to keep a grin on my face until it was time to go eat.

God's Vision Confirmed

We were destined to eat at a restaurant named Pappadeaux. It was a seafood restaurant. I was game, too. On the way to eat, Alfonzo, Nissa, and Ericka reminisced about the past. It was funny to sit there and watch them catch up. I started to see Ericka in a new light. She wasn't the bougie girl she'd seemed to be. Nissa's friend was down to earth, friendly, and lively. She looked young, but she was older than me. I was amazed at her southern dialect. I did not want her to stop talking. Besides everything else, she had the most gorgeous smile. I started to notice how well she communicated with her accent. She was so funny.

When we made it to Pappadeaux, everyone ordered their food. I remember kidding with Ericka. I told her she was going to have to pay for my dinner or we were all going to have to wash dishes. She eyed me with a look that meant, "This dude is cheap!" She did not know I was trying to ease my way into talking to her more. I could tell she was not interested in me, but she maintained that southern hospitality. Ericka and I took a picture together at dinner. I thought I was breaking ground with her, but again, she was just being nice.

The night was getting late, and it was time for us to go. Everyone had a busy schedule the next day so we took Ericka home. We all said our goodbyes. Plans were made to get together one final time before Alfonzo and Nissa headed back home to Chicago. A vision came upon me as we were leaving Ericka's home. I told my cousin and his wife, "I think I met my wife tonight."

Nissa instantly got defensive about her friend. She said, "Ericka is a God-fearing woman. She is career-oriented, and she does not have time for playing games." She also said her friend was celibate. I felt discouraged at first. I knew what my lustful motives were, but the vision never left me. I knew I met my wife that evening.

God's Vision Prepped

I had no intentions of settling down in Texas. However, there was something about this woman. Ericka was like a light that came on in my head. I could not get her out of my mind. Maybe I was a little off by telling Nissa I met my wife. I had to get to know this woman a little more. Honestly, I was not ready for Ericka. Truth be told, I had a lot of things about myself I had to work on.

That didn't stop me though. The next day, I must've sent Nissa a hundred text messages. I asked her what her friend thought about me. Nissa said Ericka thought I was cute and had nice eyebrows, but that 's all. I thought, *That's It!?* I persistently sent more texts. I had no clue why my interest grew for this woman, but I couldn't give up that easy.

Later that week the women invited me over to Ericka's to watch movies. The woman I no longer viewed as a bougie girl did not ask me over to get to know me. She only did it because she felt sorry for me. I was in a big city and didn't really know anyone. The southern hospitality in her came out again.

I accepted the invitation. I knew Alfonzo and Nissa would soon be headed back to Chicago for good. This was my chance to at least break the ice with Ericka. She gave me her telephone number. It was for calling her when I just wanted to hang out and visit local sites. The rest is history, because Ericka and I texted each other back and forth the whole night. I felt she was warming up to me, but she still remained firm in regards to us staying only friends. God was really setting me up for something big.

God's Plan Ready

Outside of working on building a relationship with Ericka, I was a loner. When it was time to get out and see more of Texas, I traveled alone to a few clubs or happy hour venues. I was always unaccompanied when I went out. I did not want anyone holding me back when I wanted to leave a certain place. Even though I was in Dallas where things were lively at times, my joy of the club life was starting to fade.

I was not as interested in partying as I was in Minnesota. I think I burned myself out going out to different social establishments in my early twenties. Everything seemed to be the same each night. Besides, I went those places to meet women. I did not drink and I definitely did not dance.

My good friend and co-worker Norman finally made it to town to work at the branch I worked at. We became roommates. Norman also had to get adjusted to Texas life so I was not alone. During this time, Ericka and I still continued to communicate as friends. We became so cool that I offered to cook dinner for her before she left town. She planned a trip home to Louisiana to visit her family for the 2006-2007 holiday season.

The "bait" instead of the date was set after she told me one of her favorite dishes. She loved Italian noodles so I made penne pasta with Alfredo sauce and some cut, grilled chicken. Dinner was served. I genuinely wanted Ericka to enjoy the food, but I thought there would be something more between us after dinner. I wanted something sweet. We had some dessert, but not what I was looking for. In simple terms, Ericka was hip to my game. She remained firm, not breaking a sweat.

God's Plan: The Education

After dinner Ericka and I hung out to talk. She immediately let me know there was not going to be anything else going on. If I had sex on my mind, that plan was destroyed. This was a good time for us to continue to get to know each other. I told her more about my life and my running days. I mentioned how close I was with my mother.

She sat there and listened to me. Ericka told me I had an interesting story and that my life was a good testimony. I nodded off her comments thinking that it was just life. We all go through something in our time here on earth. She then asked me some questions I'll never forget.

"Michael, are you saved?"

"Yes," I told her quickly.

"Would you go to heaven if you died?"

"Yes."

"How do you know you are saved?"

"I've never been to jail. I haven't killed anyone, and I am a good person." I sat still as she continued.

"Do you sin?"

"No," I replied matter-of-factly. Ericka sat there patiently and listened to me. I then told her I knew some scriptures we used to repeat in my high school track and field days. They were Proverbs 3:5-6, Matthew 6:9-13, and Philippians 4:13.

She could have turned away from, me but she didn't. She knew I was not saved and just as sinful as I could be. Ericka told me in a very gentle way, "Everyone sins and falls short of God's standards." She then explained my answers on being saved, going to heaven, and not being a sinner were all wrong. God placed it on her heart to teach me what the word "saved" meant and the true meaning of The Gospel.

"Michael," she began again. "Being saved means believing in the birth, the death, and the resurrection of Jesus Christ."

I had to know and accept this truth with all of my heart. She taught that Jesus died and paid the full price for the sins of all humanity. Once I accepted this truth, Jesus Christ would be my personal Lord and Savior.

The answer was so simple that I wanted to learn more. I had no clue what was happening in my life at that moment. Ericka told me that Jesus wanted to heal me from the inside out and have a personal relationship with me. She then grabbed her study Bible and informed me what the scriptures I'd quoted to her indicated.

I had no idea what they truly meant in high school. However, as an adult I was now grasping the words of God like I'd never heard them before. I was amazed at what she was teaching me. I wanted to learn more about scriptures. I told Ericka I had to get a copy of that same study Bible.

At a time when I would usually run from someone talking about God, I was pulled toward His word. I was like a fish on a hook. I could not break away. I was caught by God, and I was getting ready to be gutted from the inside out. I did not realize it right away. My motives were still bad. While I chased after Ericka's goods, God was right there chasing after me. He was reeling me in slowly.

God's Plan: The Invitation

To be honest, Ericka was not that interested in me. We were cool, but there were no fireworks going on between us. She did not see me the way I saw her. Her standards wouldn't be lowered either.

During one of our conversations she mentioned, "If I date anyone, he has to have a personal and intimate relationship with God, the Father." I had every opportunity to leave Ericka alone at this point, but I could not. She was constantly on my mind and heart.

After 2007 began, I thought I was making more ground with Ericka. I just knew she would soon give in to me. When she came back in town from her holiday trip, she told me that she missed me while she was visiting her family.

Soon, Ericka and I were meeting up many Sundays to go to church together. She attended a mega church in Grand Prairie. My apartment complex was not too far from it.

That's it! I thought, *Maybe if I tell Ericka I finally have that relationship with God, I could have her the way I want.* I was wrong again, because she would not compromise her bond with her heavenly Father. I knew God had to be laughing at me, too. He had invested so much in Ericka's spiritual life so that she could gradually change mine. Ericka knew what she wanted. It was to be married to a husband who sincerely followed Christ. She took her walk with God very seriously. She was my example of a strong Christian.

I admired her faith when we sat next to each other at church. Every time I went, I always thought the pastor talked about me in his sermons. The more I started reading God's word, the more my heart grew fonder for Christ. The messages I received each Sunday were tugging at my heart. The word of God was a mirror showing me just how corrupt I was on the inside and out. I still avoided many invitations to give my life to Christ. I was fighting myself, because I did not want to change my ways and bad habits.

One Sunday in June 2007, I was not able to struggle with God anymore. I could not avoid the special invitation given to me. The altar call was made as usual during service. Just when I thought church was going to be over, the opportunity of Christ's invitation was extended a little longer. In my heart, something was pulling me to accept the request. I could not move.

Ericka turned to me and gave me the warmest look. She whispered, "I will walk with you to the altar." I stood there in total fear still not moving. Then something hit me. Before I knew it, I made my way toward the front of the mega church. My head was bowed down. Ericka stood right beside me. To my surprise some of her close friends also came and stood with me.

I finally submitted my life to Jesus Christ. I was very scared though, because I did not know what to do next. Even though I didn't know how to proceed, God did. He was already in the transformation process. All I had to do was accept Jesus Christ as my Lord and Savior, and He would do the rest.

Divine Orchestration: The Chiseling Process

I would like to say that my life instantly changed when I gave it to Jesus Christ, but that was not the case to me. I did not realize there was a process taking place in my life after I accepted Christ. There was a lot spiritual warfare that took place in me after my altar call experience. I continued trying to break Ericka down and cause destruction in her life, but God was not going to allow it. No matter how hard I pressured Ericka, she remained right by my side through the battles. God and Ericka would not let me go no matter what I did.

During this time I reflected on my past. In my life I was used to running and going from one place to the next. Sometimes others determined which lane I would run in,

Michael Layne

other times I changed lanes on my own during life. God knew where He wanted me though. He was doing something for my own good. I realized I could not run anymore. I had to let my heavenly Father decide my course. He was doing things His way anyway.

Part of being coached by God meant following that same vision He gave me when I first met Ericka. It was all in His master plan. On November 4, 2007, I took a step toward that vision when I first laid eyes on Ericka. In our normal routine of going to church, God placed it on my heart to ask Ericka to marry me. I wondered, *Now, how I was going to propose to her?*

I had no plan in place. I wasn't discouraged though, because I knew God had already invested so much in me. If he showed me the woman who would become my wife, I trusted he would provide the way to ask her.

After thinking about different scenarios, He provided a way for me . . . Again! I decided not to take Ericka out to dinner and pop the big question there. Instead I did something that was far from traditional and out of the ordinary. I strategized a plan to propose in a place that was very familiar to me. I took her to a local track and field near her home.

When we got on the track, I immediately grabbed her hand and walked her to lane number one. As we were walking in the first lane, I began talking. I told her how much track and field and running meant to me. I said, "It taught me so much regarding life. I learned about victory and defeat. There was training, discipline, and sacrifice. There were competitors against me and family and friends who supported me."

I knew she was listening so I continued. "There were times when I didn't want to train and times when I needed to train. I discovered the endurance I had to have and the ups and the downs in competition. Contending in track and field compares to life on so many levels."

Before Ericka and I could complete a full lap in lane one, Ericka then asked me, "How long are we going to walk on this track?" Her patience was growing thin, because she only had on her flip flops. "We won't be long," I replied. When we approached the starting line, I told her, "The track goes on and on because it's a circle." She already knew this but the thing about competing in track and field was that I also had teammates. I then mentioned, "Ericka, I want you to be my teammate on this circle of life."

I got on my knees on the starting line to symbolize the start of something new in our lives. I took out the ring I had just bought and looked into her eyes. I then asked, "Will you marry me?" She shed a tear in her eye, and exclaimed, "Yes!" Ericka explained that years prior to me moving to Texas, she often walked this same track. She said "I used to have one-on-one praying time with God. I asked Him to send me a husband."

She cried, but it wasn't only because she was happy about my proposal. It was also because her prayers were being answered *at the exact same place* she prayed to God. An answered prayer for her, a blessing to me, and God did not stop there . . .

To Be Continued

For by grace you have been saved through faith; and that not of yourselves it is the gift of God; not as a result of works, so that no one may boast. For we are His workmanship, created in Christ Jesus for good works, which God prepared beforehand so that we would walk in them. Ephesians 2: 8-10 (NASB)

Mike's Gospel Playlist

1. "Run 'Til I Finish" by Smokie Norful
2. "For The Good of Them" by Rev. Milton Brunson & TCC ft/Kim McFarland
3. "In My Name" by Rev. Milton Brunson & TCC ft/ Kim McFarland
4. "More Than Anything" by Lamar Campbell and Spirit Of Praise
5. "I Smile" by Kirk Franklin
6. "God Favored Me" by Hezekiah & LFC
7. "Grace Of God" by Sheri Jones-Moffett
8. "Beautiful Things" by Gungor
9. "Available To You" by Rev. Milton Brunson & TCC
10. "Hear My Call" by Jill Scott
11. "Say A Prayer" by Donald Lawrence ft/Faith Evans
12. "He's Preparing Me" by Daryl Coley
13. "He Has His Hands On You" by Marvin Sapp
14. "I Will Run" by Freddy Rodriguez
15. "You Called Me Friend" by Fred Hammond
16. "Your Steps Are Ordered" by Fred Hammond

And many, many more . . .